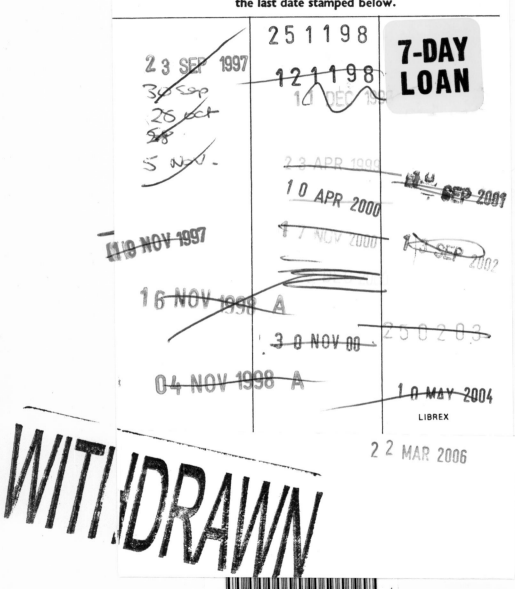

NEIL LYNDON

NO MORE SEX WAR

The Failures of Feminism

SINCLAIR–STEVENSON

First published in Great Britain by
Sinclair-Stevenson
7/8 Kendrick Mews
London SW7 3HG England

Copyright © 1992 by Neil Lyndon

British Library Cataloguing in Publication Data
A CIP catalogue record for this book is available from the British Library.

ISBN: 1 85619 191 5

Typeset by Deltatype Ltd, Ellesmere Port

Printed and bound in Great Britain by Clays Ltd, St Ives plc

For
John Alexander Lyndon

− in the hope that it might make sense
to him one day
♀ ♂

Contents

Acknowledgements

Sinclair-Stevenson and the author wish to thank the following who have kindly given permission for the use of copyright material:

Ashley Montague for *The Natural Superiority of Women* (reprinted with the permission of Macmillan Publishing company from *The Natural Superiority of Women* by Ashley Montague. Copyright 1953 and renewed © 1981 by Ashley Montague).
Betty Friedan for *The Feminine Mystique*, published in Britain by Victor Gollancz Ltd, 1963
Germaine Greer for *The Female Eunuch*, published by MacGibbon & Kee Ltd 1970; and for *The Madwoman's Underclothes*, published by Picador Books, 1986
Jane McLoughlin for *The Demographic Revolution*, published by Faber & Faber, 1991
Woman in Sexist Society, ed. Vivian Gorrick and Barbara K. Moran, published by Basic Books Inc., USA, 1971
Trevor Jones, Brian Maclean and Jock Young for *The Islington Crime Survey* published by Gower Publishing Co Ltd, Ashgate Publishing, © Centre for Criminology at Middlesex Polytechnic 1986
Sheila Rowbotham for *The Past is Before Us* published by Penguin, 1988
Susan S.M. Edwards for *Policing 'Domestic' Violence* published by Sage Publications Ltd 1989
Chiswick Family Rescue for permission to quote from its 'Key Principles', 1990
HMSO for the 'Report of the Inquiry into Child Abuse in Cleveland', 1987
The Times, the *Independent*, the *Independent Magazine*, the *London Review of Books*, *Monthly Review*, *Radio Times*, *Arena* and *Time Out* for permission to quote from published articles.

A number of authors and public bodies refused permission to quote from their works in this book. They and their works were:

Rosalind Miles for *The Rites of Man* published by Grafton Books

Rosalind Miles & Anne Kelleher for BBC 2's *Fighting Talk*

Andrea Dworkin for *Mercy* published by Martin Secker & Warburg

London Rape Crisis Centre for *Sexual Violence: The Reality for Women* published by The Women's Press

Nell Dunn for *Talking to Women* published by MacGibbon & Kee Ltd

Kate Millett for *Sexual Politics* published by Virago

Robin Morgan (ed) for *Sisterhood is Powerful*

Prologue

A lot of gender switching goes on in this book. None of it, I trust, is irreversible. It is all done for effect. At many points, I ask the reader to imagine the impact of words or sentiments if they are taken out of the mouth of a man and given to a woman; or vice versa. Sometimes, this exercise in mental transvestism is requested so frequently in brief passages that the reader will find that he or she has only just struggled into the frock when he or she is asked to put on the codpiece. If these efforts get confusing or wearisome – or result in your wearing a codpiece over the frock – I apologise.

I urge the reader to carry this mental device along as a bookmark. I ask you to apply it to your author. If, at any point, you find yourself saying 'That's a typical man talking' or 'Only a man would say that' or 'I wonder what's gone wrong with this bloke that he should hold such strange opinions', I ask you to work the wonder of the gender switch and see what might have been your reaction if my words had been written by a woman.

Some touches of autobiography are given in this book, usually to flesh out historical passages. Otherwise the book is an argument, often abstract, containing little which is directly personal to me (in fact, I did consider naming it 'Nothing Personal: The Failures of Feminism', partly in response to the standard feminist line which claims that 'the personal is political' and which, to my mind, has caused little change to be effected in those dimensions of political life which are impersonal). The book emerges, most certainly, from my life in the years 1965–91; but I would like to think that I treat the experience of those decades as being universal, shared in some measure by members of my generation (I was born in 1946) and by immediately surrounding generations.

During those years, I have had some troubles of my own with women; and a number of women, I know, would say that they have had trouble with and from me. Some of those troubles grew out of the events and social changes which are described in this book; but my interpretation of those events is not, I hope, driven exclusively by personal history. An interviewer on a television programme once said that I seemed to be very bitter and allowed me no time to reply. My answer would have been that, if I am bitter, it is not for myself. I am disappointed to the soles of my boots that my generation, which promised so much, should have delivered so little by way of radical change in the institutions of state, in the rights and freedoms of individuals, should have made so little difference to the slavery of worthless work which millions of our fellow citizens endure and to the privations and squalors among which we live.

Much of the responsibility for that conspicuous failure I attribute to the influence of feminism and to the perverted account of personal relations and of social composition which feminism has fostered. To my way of thinking, the cardinal tenets of feminism divided my generation, effectively disempowering and disenfranchising its members. It does make me bitterly angry that my generation, which prided itself so complacently on its soul, on its powers of intelligence and analysis, should have fallen so cloddishly for totalitarian simplicities which declared a war of eternal opposition between men and women. *There* is a score which I am eager to settle; but it isn't personal.

2

These points are among the conclusions towards which I reach throughout the book and especially in its closing chapters. In order to get there, I have had to track back across the last quarter of a century, questioning all the assumptions which became common to the time and which were lodged in my own mind.

The book as a whole is, therefore, a ponder which I invite you to follow and to share. It results from the countless hundreds of hours of thought I have given, God help me, to the feminist commonplaces of our culture and of our times. Those commonplaces have come my way as they have come your way – through books, through articles in newspapers and magazines, over the airwaves of radio and television and in arguments in homes and pubs and offices. We all share the culture of those commonplaces. I approach it not as a scholar but as a citizen who has had this culture imposed upon him and as a journalist who is eager to observe and to record the dimensions of a contemporary phenomenon. We may not, at the beginning of this book, share the light in which I see that phenomenon. I trust that we may have drawn nearer to a shared view by the end of the book. The motto or rubric of this book might be 'I question: may we doubt?'. The work thus runs as a discussion between me and my experience and as an argument between you and me. I propose. You dispose. You're the governor.

To that end, I want to offer the reader a sure and certain point of departure. Here follows a short list of facts which I ask you to keep at the back of your mind through all the chapters which follow. I shall be returning to them, frequently, for commentary and amplification; but let me just put them down now, straightforwardly and simply, as foundation stones for the discussion which is to come.

*   Until the autumn of 1991, when the Children Act

became law, the fathers of at least one in every four children born in Great Britain had no rights with regard to those children.

Approximately 175,000 children are born every year to unmarried women. Those women have had all the rights of parenthood for those children. The men have had no legal rights of paternity. They might not even register the birth of their baby. The mother might, with unchallengeable legal authority, refuse the father any right to see or to be with his child and remove the children to another place, even to another country, without his consent. The Children Act is intended to afford to unmarried fathers the right to acquire parental responsibility on the same terms as married fathers; but we cannot, at present, guess how its vaguely expressed terms will work in practice.

* A man who makes an application to the divorce court for joint custody of the children of a broken marriage has a one-in-five chance of success. A man who makes an application for sole custody of his children has a one-in-ten chance of success.

About 175,000 divorces are granted in Great Britain every year. In more than 100,000 of those divorces, the couples have children under the age of sixteen. The routine practice of the divorce courts of Great Britain is to strip men of their property and income and, simultaneously, deny them equal rights of access and care for their children.

* About 200,000 abortions are legally effected in Great Britain every year. We do not know how many of the fathers of those foetuses might have wished to see their children born: nobody has ever tried to count them. They are not accorded a glimmer of public

4

attention nor an atom of legal rights. Subject only to the consent of doctors, the pregnant woman is given the absolute right to choose to abort the foetus, regardless of the father's wishes or the state of their relationship when she conceived. The inseminating man has no right, in law or in convention, to express or to record an opinion on the abortion, even if the woman has previously openly and unambiguously expressed the desire to bear their child.

* About 700,000 babies are born in the UK every year. The 700,000 men who are their fathers have no right in law to time off work when those babies are born.

* A man may not be classed as a dependant for social security benefits in Great Britain.

* Widowers who are left with the care of children are not entitled to the state benefits which a widow would receive.

* Though it will soon be changed, the law in Great Britain still allows women to retire and receive a state pension at the age of sixty while requiring men to work until they are sixty-five. The coming change in the law has been imposed upon Britain to bring the country into line with its European partners. The protests of men on this incontestable point of inequality have been ignored in Britain for twenty-five years.

Two connected consequences flow from this list. First, it gives an unusual perspective upon our times and the societies in which we live: it shifts the focus of the light in which we see ourselves. Second – and more importantly, in my mind – it must mean, in each of its particular parts and in

5

sum, that the cardinal tenets of feminism add up to a totem of bunkum.

First, let's adjust our eyes to a different angle of light.

Throughout the whole of this century and especially in the last twenty-five years, Western societies have been extensively preoccupied with the changing position of women. The movement to adjust society to accommodate those changes, to alter the civic and political standing of women and to afford them legal and financial equality has been, incomparably, the most important single force for social reform in this century.

We can now see – it follows from that list – that with the focus of reforming light and zeal being directed upon the position of women, a shadow or penumbra of neglect has fallen upon the realities of life for men and upon the social terms and conditions by which men's personal and family lives are extensively defined and limited. Their common difficulties and their universal and institutionalised disadvantages have been overlooked. Or, where those disadvantages have been acknowledged, the prevailing tendency has been to act as if they must count for nothing – as if any difficulties shared by men must necessarily be trivial blights on the lives of weak individuals compared with the imposing grievances shared by all women.

Men, it has been broadly agreed, would be exhibiting an unseemly ingratitude, unmanly and unsoldierly, if they were to moan and whine about their troubles.

But those troubles are not so trivial. Take another look at that list. Each point touches upon the marrow of an individual's life – the main issues of life and death, of love and sex, of marriage and work, of the very rights of man as a citizen and as a creature of family. After the abolition of slavery, can any human right, any civic issue, be more essential than the right of a parent to live with her or his

6

child, as best they can hack out their own domestic arrangements? No society which abrogates, abridges, compromises
or neglects that right for hundreds of thousands of individuals who have nothing in common but their gender may
advance a secure claim to be working towards the expunc-
tion of sexual prejudices and inequalities.

Even so, the main issue here is not the seriousness of the
particular grievances on that list; nor is it the overall picture
which it relays of routine, systemic and institutionalised
disadvantage for men. Each of those disadvantages is an
element of fissive material which can be bound together to
make a grenade. If the assembled device is lobbed over the
ramparts so that it drops deep into the foundations of
modern feminism, it may blow up that towering edifice of
bullshit, that babel of intolerance and casuistry which has
cast a murrain on the life of the West in the last quarter of
this century.

During the last twenty-five years, we have all grown
accustomed to the propositions of the feminism which took
its origins in the New Left of America and Europe in the later
Sixties. The corner-piece of that mosaic of belief, assertion
and argument has been the claim that all post-nomadic
societies have been 'patriarchal'. This ought to mean that all
modern societies have been organised to endorse the powers
of the father-figure; but it means more than that in the
terminology of modern feminism. It means that those
societies have been organised by men for the benefit of men
and to the disadvantage of women.

We have all, in some measure, paid lip-service to the
pseudo-Marxist tenets of modern feminism. We have all
gone along with the general presumption that women belong
by birth to a social and economic class which is oppressed by
the patriarchal system as it is operated by a social and
economic class composed, by birth, of men.

Now we can see and assert that those propositions are false at root. It cannot be true that men oppress women in a system which they devise for their benefit if, in a number of vital and central elements of the lives of men, they find themselves in positions of disadvantage compared with women. The proposition cannot be squared with the evidence.

You must make what you will of that evidence. You may feel free to say that men, evidently, don't care about their children. You may share the opinion of a woman visiting my family house and admiring it who said, 'Houses are for women and children, not for those with dangly bits.' You may take the view that men, being barely sub-human, uncivilised, barbaric, slobbish, undependable, unfamilial, need to be kept in their place by a system of law and regulation which confers them with rights of paternity on strictly limited terms.

You can say what you like but you cannot say that we live in a patriarchal system which is designed to protect and to promote the advantages of men over women. Can you see why that line is insupportable? Are you with me?

If the point is not self-evident, let me bash it into shape.

We all understand that the system of apartheid in South Africa was devised to sustain and to ensure the political and social supremacy of the white minority. The denial of political rights to blacks and the other circumscribing conditions in which they lived all added up to a simple division of races in which whites had all power and blacks had none.

The system could not have been described as a white supremacy, apartheid would have had no meaning, if blacks had been able to exercise rights and powers which were denied to whites. If, for instance, blacks had been allowed to vote while whites were denied that right, the very idea of a white supremacist society would have been preposterous.

8

Do you see what I am driving at?

The same logic, applied to the facts I have advanced, explodes the feminist myth of male supremacist patriarchy in Western societies. If any disadvantages apply to all men, if any individual man is denied a right by reason of his gender which is afforded to every individual woman, then it must follow that ours is not a society which is exclusively devised to advance and protect advantages for men over women.

It is not a patriarchy.

I want to argue that, since it is demonstrably unreasonable, the false feminist picture can only be sustained through the exercise of intolerance, vulgar prejudice and totalitarianism in thought and speech. I want to try to show that the picture of men which is broadly shared and agreed throughout our society can be contested in every detail, in all its parts and as a whole. I want to advance the opinion that the feminist world-picture came into being, in the first place, not as a tool of progress and a weapon of liberation but as a restrictive force which refused and inhibited change. I want to say that we have all, women and men, been harmed in our personal lives and in our political potentialities, as citizens, by that reactionary world-view. A great number of the correctable wrongs and deficiencies in our societies, I argue, have been deepened by feminism; and the power of its ideology has, in my view, inhibited and diminished the political powers of my generation, now thirty, forty and fifty something, now at the pinnacle of what ought to be their political powers but, in effect, neutralised.

That feminist world-view was always, in my book, a force of troubled and troubling reaction. If you, the reader, take that world-view as given, if it is the essential foundation of your self-esteem, if you take it for granted that women have

9

had to struggle to advance their liberation against an oppressive system and that the changes which have occurred in the position of women in the last twenty years are the crowning jewel of achievement for the libertarian and liberationist generation of the Sixties, then the argument and discussion between us is likely to be a hot and heavy tussle.

Before we get at it, I must pick up a couple of banana skins which have been strewn in the path of this argument, apparently to ensure that nobody should go far upon it. The fruitiest and most rotten of these is the presumption that anybody who voices doubts or disquiets about modern feminism and its claims must be misogynistic, must be waging war upon women as a whole, must wish to see women returned to the domestic ghetto of life as it was lived by women before the mid-Sixties. That accusation has often been aimed at me in the last three years, thrown up in a barrage of flak which has come my way since I began to express my views in public.

Like other accusations (he cannot know what he is talking about; he can't have read enough; there must be something wrong with him; he's just trying to score a buck), the misogynist charge seems to be nothing more than a device, like tinsel paper in the air, to divert accurate navigation on the subject.

It is perfectly illogical to say that somebody who espouses anti-feminist beliefs must be anti-woman. It makes no more sense than it would to say that an anti-Nazi must be anti-German or an anti-Communist must be anti-Russian. The subject of this book is a body of abstract belief, which may or may not amount to an ideology but is most decidedly viewed by its adherents as a faith. Viewed in that light, feminism has no better claim to absolute truth than any other ideology or faith; and it ought to be equally open to scrutiny and argument.

10

Feminists do make a habit of advancing the claim, explicitly or implicitly, to represent all women. Clare Short's 1991 book *Dear Clare*, for example, is subtitled: *this is what women feel about Page Three*. The book is, in fact, a compilation of letters from some hundreds of women who feel distressed by or hostile to the semi-nude photographs of young women on the pages of tabloid newspapers. Many women, we know, are not at all aggrieved or distressed by those photographs. Clare Short is not, therefore, entitled to say that her book represents women: it represents nothing more than a body of opinion, which may be extensive and may comprise many women. The implicit claim in the sub-title illustrates the totalitarian habits of mind of feminists. They *say* they speak for women: to their way of thinking, it follows that anybody who argues with them is arguing against the interests of all women.

That solecism will be deployed against this book. I urge the reader to beware and to be armed with a rudimentary distinction: an anti-feminist argument is not necessarily anti-woman.

As the argument in this book unfolds, I trust the reader will see that a vital element of its case against feminism is the failure, as I see it, of that body of belief to supply whole and happy answers to the dilemmas of women in our age. The book is neither an attack on women nor a defence of men. It is, rather, an attempt to argue that modern feminism has led us into a misprision of the history of our age and a misconstruction of the essential interests of men and women.

Those interests are, to my mind, nearly always identical and always symmetrical. It follows that they are equal in value and that the rights of individual men and women ought to be equal in law and social practice. If you slip on another nasty banana skin of unreason deposited on the path of argument by feminists, you may suppose – as they do – that anybody who argues against feminism is, automatically, an opponent of equal rights for women.

Beware again: it ain't necessarily so. Your author is wholly and unreservedly in favour of equality between men and women in all social, civic and familial rights. Your author wishes to see as many women as men at work, in positions of office and authority. Your author doesn't give a damn whether women or men wear skirts or trousers, high heels or builders' boots. I am no more distressed than you by the sight of a woman in the presidential limousine or a man in rouge or a pinafore. I do wonder whether the social changes that have resulted in those spectacles have much, if anything, to do with the claims of modern feminists who have appropriated them as trophies of triumph. If we can agree that it is permissible to wonder, we can get on with the argument. Let me say that, from my side, no holds are barred. Shall we get at it?

ONE

——

Incubus

'All men are Idi Amin,' said the hostess.

My jaw may have dropped.

'Are you serious?' I said.

'Of course they are,' she said. 'All men have within them that blood-lust, that sadistic pleasure in inflicting torture. What's the matter: why are you looking at me like that?'

'Can't you see how damaging it is to say that?'

'Oh, pooh,' she said, 'that old line again. I'm sick of hearing how damaging the truth is to the fragile male ego, how careful we must be not to upset them . . .'

'That's not what I meant,' I said. 'I mean that it must be damaging to you and your reputation for sanity to say such a thing. You can't say that all men are Idi Amin any more than you can say that all Jews are mean [the lady was a Jew and she bridled], all West Indians smell or all Pakistanis are good at business. It makes you look like an idiot.'

The year was, I believe, 1976; but it might have been 1975 or 1977. The party was being given in the hostess's house in one of the most fashionable crescents in north London. She was and is a very well respected editor of literary journals which command extensive influence in intellectual fashion. The party was jammed with her famous friends, including writers, movie directors and film stars, publishers and their editors, scholars and style-makers. It was a gathering of the kind which was regularly parodied in cartoon strips and satirical snips in *Private Eye* – giving the picture of a

13

closely knit establishment of media trendies. The picture, in this case, was broadly true.

In the moment when we turned away from each other, I first realised that a wretched intolerance had entered the atmosphere of a wide society and was becoming an orthodox aspect of our times, even in circles, like this party, where it might have been expected to be inadmissible. If you tried to isolate one distinguishing characteristic of the mental attitudes of all the guests in that house, it might have been that they prided themselves on their intellectual flexibility and tolerance, the refinements of their powers of scepticism which gave them a sure immunity to totalitarianism. All their habits of mind and speech eschewed categorical certainties. These people were professional doubters, distinguishers and collectors of subtleties.

None of them would ever have said 'All women are Myra Hyndley' or 'All women are the Dowager Empress Cixi' (well, Martin Amis might; but you'd know that he was just pushing it). None of them, even if they had entertained such a notion, would take it seriously or let it become – as that lady editor would and did – an underlying principle in her future journalistic work and commissioning of articles. In any case, even if fashion had allowed, they would have to be drunk to admit an expression so unambiguous. The single phrase which most often punctuated their speech and writing was 'in a sense'; rarely 'absolutely'; never 'right on'. The lady was not saying 'In a sense, all men are Idi Amin' (had she done so, this book might never have been written). She was saying 'All men are Idi Amin absobleedinglutely.'

I had come of age among the absolutelys and the right-ons. In the new left circles of the late Sixties and early Seventies in Britain, I has witnessed the spread of absolute assertions

14

of categorical evils in men. The givers of parties I attended in a commune house in Dalston in 1970/71 might well have said that 'all men are Idi Amin' and many of the guests might, if they had been capable of coherent speech, have assented. But those people were, evidently, off the wall of British society. Some of them believed that the Provisional IRA represented a force for revolutionary liberation in Ireland. Some of them believed that the election of Richard Nixon in the 1972 Presidential election would hasten the collapse of liberalism and bring closer the revolution in Amerika, as they liked to call it. Most of them believed that a proletariat existed in Britain and would rise to bring revolution. They were young assholes who didn't know what they were talking about and, as was their due, they got little notice or attention from the wider society with which, in any case, they were supposed to be at war.

In my mind, it never counted two bits if the Dalston bandilleros held men, as a generality and commonalty, in contempt, sharing the view that men constituted a repressive class to which distinctive and primaeval ills inhered. To my way of thinking, however, it mattered greatly if a prosperous hostess, leader of intellectual style and of fashionable attitude, shared the same habits of thought as the fraggle-heads down East and felt free to give them vent in her imposing house just off Regent's Park, in the bosom of her society of establishment figures and directors of trend.

It meant that an incubus was covering the time, penetrating the minds even of those who had most distinguished degrees of intellectual discernment upon which to depend for their self-esteem. It meant that some of the very cleverest and most influential people among us might surrender their minds to a genus of totalitarianism. It struck me as being a moment such as might have occurred in the salons beside the River Moskva in 1927 or along the Unter den Linden in

1932, when the pronunciamentos of totalitarianisms were given place on the cultivated lips of the intelligentsia: a moment when an outsider might have realised that a broad society was deeply infected and that its promise was spoiled.

The idea that all men are Idi Amin never became a central proposition of government, though I shall argue that it has affected the counsels of ministers of state. It was never implemented and executed to cause the deaths of tens of millions of citizens, though I shall argue that it had bearing on the destruction of a host of millions of foetuses. It never became a cardinal point of opposition between nation states, resulting in mass mobilisations and years of total war, though I shall argue that the sex war to which it appeared to give legitimacy did harm to the personal lives of millions. There *is* a drastic point of absolute difference between the scale and effects of the totalitarianisms of the different ages of the century; and I affirm that difference. The totalitarianism which allowed the hostess to say that all men are Idi Amin happens to have been our very own, the one we have cultivated and lived with – tamer, more cerebral and more domesticated as our times have been.

In following years, down to 1988, I kept half an ear and a passing eye on this trend while removing myself progressively from the society which it most directly influenced: I moved out of London, kept away from smart parties, lived and worked abroad. Physical removal and exclusion did not, however, confer immunity. The prejudices of totalitarianism were in the air, mediated through broadcasts and newspapers. The incubus was in the atmosphere of our age. Constantly changing shape and form, expressed through a host of voices private and public, this incubus was a moving and irresistible force. Opposition to it was denied; argument refused. A man was not entitled to answer. 'This is an argument you *cannot* win,' as one of my feminist lovers told me in 1970. There was nothing to do but keep your head down and hope that the incubus would pass over while we were still alive.

By the end of the Eighties, I felt that I had had enough. I was in my mid-forties. I had a young son. My entire adult life had been spent under the influence of this poisonous orthodoxy, in the grains and cells of which was the axiomatic presumption that I and all other men, regardless of our own tastes and opinions, regardless of our own conduct and our own desires, regardless of whether we were sexually promiscuous or wholly celibate, regardless of whether we were loving fathers, attentive and dutiful husbands, loyal and honourable colleagues and employers or employees, were enemies of women. Were my son's infancy and adulthood to be blighted by these poisons?

The end of the line and the real beginning of this book came, for me, in a shabbily furnished and stale-smelling hotel room in the north-east of England. The trail could hardly have removed me further from the salons of Regent's Park.

On the 1st July 1991, I was staying in Hartlepool where I was working on a magazine article. After breakfast in my hotel room I switched on the television, hoping to catch the 9.00 a.m. news bulletin, and, as the picture came into focus, these were the first words I heard:

'I think men are pretty useless, to tell the truth.'

A woman author – I didn't get her name – was being interviewed on TV-AM's 'After Nine' show. The subject, I gathered, was something to do with the family and with the division and apportionment of domestic labour. The interviewer asked the author if her own husband was useless. She laughed and said words which I did not take down but which were to the effect: oh, no: I make an exception of him; I'm talking about men in general.

Before I went to sleep the previous night, I had been reading the last chapters of *The Rites of Man* by Rosalind Miles, published in the spring of 1991. Among the passages and sentences I noted from that book was one where she claimed that more men go to see their doctors for consultations about impotence than for any other illness or medical concern. Later in the book, Dr Miles asserts that maleness itself is the key to violent acts committed by men. She says that, because the common feature among violent offenders is their maleness, the explanation for violence and any hope for its cure must be sought in the nature and essence of that gender.

(That passage towards the end of the book fits with one of Rosalind Miles's opening declarations in the Prologue where she says that if you can explain violence, you can explain man and, it follows in her mind, if you can explain masculinity, you can explain violence.)

You may say that anybody who chooses for his bedtime reading a book with the subtitle *Love, Sex and Death in the Making of the Male*, rather than *A Guide to Hartlepool* or the *Gideon's Bible*, is asking for vexation. Only a man with a specialised taste for the octopus of chop-logic, indefensible assertion and special pleading which steals from the sunken wreck of modern feminism would put himself to sleep with *The Rites of Man*; and it may be felt that he has earned himself an uneasy slumber.

But, to switch on the television, in the half-hearted hope of catching the headlines and to be greeted with the declaration that 'men are pretty useless' is to be dealt an unsought irritation. It is, however, a moment which genuinely typifies an aspect of our days just as Rosalind Miles's totalitarianisms typify a frame of thought which influences the social and political life of the West. She is one of a legion of influential people who have got it into their heads and will say that all men are Idi Amin. Absolutely.

TWO

Typical Men; and the Women Who Name Them

The lady writer on the TV felt free to say that 'men are pretty useless'. The lady author between the hard covers gave it as a fact that more men consult their doctors about impotence than about any other ailment or illness.

Try switching the terms of the first of those remarks and you can instantly get a light touch of the intolerance in the atmosphere surrounding men. Try applying the tests of reason and the rules of evidence to the other remark and you can catch a potent whiff of the stink of totalitarianism.

Imagine, for instance, what the public response might be if a studio guest on a morning TV programme voiced the aside that 'Dogs are pretty useless'; or cats, horses or budgerigars; terrapins, grasshoppers or jumping fleas. Before the interviewer has time to draw breath for her next question, the telephone lines to the TV company would be blocked with indignant protesters, lovers of little companions who felt personally aggrieved by the insult to their dumb friends.

If the studio guest had said, 'Anybody under the age of ten or over the age of fifty-five is pretty useless in my opinion,' she and the television company might run some small risk of a nationwide petition being raised in defence of the dignity of the elderly or the rights of infants, which petition would be borne to Whitehall by the nimble and child-minded Mary Whitehouse and presented to Lord Rees-Mogg for investiga-

20

tion by the Broadcasting Standards Brigade of Guards (or whatever it is called).

Think, further – and here is the most telling illustration – what might happen if any man appearing on television were to say 'Women are pretty useless.' Can you imagine that any man would speak such a thought other than Sir Kingsley Amis, who seems to be proud of the pips he has been awarded as the country's Number One Misogynist? Can you imagine what would happen to any man other than Kingsley Amis if he voiced that thought on the airwaves of public transmission?

The interviewer, for a start, would be bound to give him a sharp crack across his prejudices with her clipboard. If she were Anna Ford, she might rise to some heroic display of righteous militancy such as throwing a glass of water down the interviewee's clothes. Teams of women workers at the studios might go off-line on their terminals, requiring assurances from their employers that the guest should never again be invited to express his hateful opinions. The Equal Opportunities Commission would investigate, report and chide. Clare Short would rise in the House of Commons to bring in a Bill making illegal the casual expression of demeaning thoughts about women. The Style section of the *Sunday Times* would devote its front page to an investigation into the size of the offending man's penis and the state of his marriage. All the hell, in other words, that the feminist lobby can raise would be kicked up. (I agree that, in sum, it's not a very terrifying array of sanctions compared with, say, the Official Secrets Act but it does, nonetheless, represent a body of retaliations and punishments which are consolidated, officious and automatic).

It is universally understood, after twenty years of feminist campaigning on the topic, that women are not to be demeaned by generalised insult; that their nobility and worth as individuals are not to be undermined by sneer or jibe; and that special respect must be paid to the plight and the disadvantages all women are supposed to share as members of an oppressed majority, sometimes known as a minority. Men, in other words, know that they must watch their step in speaking about women. They also know that they are not, themselves, entitled to the respect of a dog.

What followed, then, when our lady writer smirked and dismissed half of humanity as being 'pretty useless'? What challenge was she given to justify and to amplify a remark of such base and gormless vulgarity? What response did she get from her interviewer to a line of cant which pisses upon all the efforts made by all the men who devote their lives and all their waking energies to their families, all those whose principal desire is to be a good and dutiful husband and father, all those for whom the love of and for a woman is the critical and indispensable focus of desire in adult life?

She was asked if her remark applied to her husband. She said that, of course, it did not. She excepted him. The conversation moved on.

(You may be feeling that I am making a lot out of this trivial incident. I should say that I haven't yet made the half of it. The very triviality of the moment is the reason that it matters: it is a moment like any other.)

When the lady writer was asked if her husband was useless, the question meant, by extension, 'Is it true in your direct personal experience that men are useless?' Her answer declared, unambiguously, that it was not true in her direct experience that men were useless. Remembering that feminists have, throughout the last twenty-five years, insisted that personal experience is endued with political meaning, we may wonder what political deductions this woman may draw from her experience.

When she explained that she was not speaking personally

but was referring to men *in general*, her interrogation ceased. No further explanation was necessary or called for. It was perfectly okay for her to be running down a gender of humanity so long as she wasn't taking a dig at her own man nor, by implication, yours.

So why did she say it? If neither her own man nor yours should be called useless, who or what did she have in mind? And why did nobody object, protest or care that public utterance was being given to a prejudice which was without foundation even in the experience of the speaker?

The answer, I want to say, is that, by the early years of the 1990s in the West and, to my knowledge, most especially in Great Britain, many women and plenty of men felt more than free, felt *obliged*, to give vent to any irrational sliver of derision about men which darted across the frontal lobes of their brains. They were not, in so speaking, describing their own direct experience – neither, as women, of the men they lived with nor, as men, of themselves. They were describing an *other*. They were referring to a universal spectre of ill, a commonly agreed bogyman, whipping-boy and boogaboo.

A picture of this frightful man can be found in all our minds: that is where he takes his primary existence and performs his essential social role. He is the filthy sod in the thigh-high Doc Martens, torn denims and AC/DC T-shirt who hauls his snarling Rottweiler on to the underground train, drops a soiled hypodermic, lights up a stinking roll-up and belches over a can of lager. He is the one who leers over the tits in the *Sun* while he is waiting to collect his packet of dole and who passes the cash over the counters of the pub and the betting shop as soon as it is in his greasy fingers, sticking the remains up the fannies of whores. Reeling home with a head full of losses and a gut full of bitter and chips, he clamps his teeth into the carotid artery of the starving Rottweiler before he rips the rags from the back of the little woman, belabours her with the dog's studded leash and takes his prick to the anuses of his screaming children.

We do not know this horror on terms of personal acquaintance. He is not one of us; but we have agreed that he is out there somewhere and that he is the All-Man.

By the beginning of the Nineties, this other horror had become the cynosure and representative of all men. He was, by common consent, the point of all reference and the focus of all presumptions about manhood and masculinity. Men as a generalised whole (not your husband, nor hers) had become useless *and* the unspeakable evil, the object of a light smirk of dismissal and the irredeemably condemned for whom, as I am about to show, no imprecations, no damnings, no luridness of language was excessive. A large part of the point of this book is to try to get to the botom of the social conditions and the chain of events which composed that incubus and resulted in that truly extraordinary consequence; but, first, I need to go many steps further in pinning down some of its outer features.

Rosalind Miles is a particularly valuable source in this task. Hers is an authentic voice of modern feminism. She has made for herself a small but secure place among the authoritative commentators upon our age. She appears on BBC radio's 'Any Questions' and on BBC television's 'Question Time'. She has been given the opportunity to make documentary programmes for television, such as one which was transmitted in 1991 on the so-called disadvantages of women in the so-called male system of justice. In April 1991, she was interviewed alone for half an hour on a late-afternoon BBC television programme called 'Fighting Talk', giving her views on the state of modern feminism.

She is, in other words, recognised as an authority. Implicit in that recognition is a broad presumption that her views have been carefully composed in study, that they add up to a body of reason and that they make sense. She would not, otherwise, be invited to sit on the panel of 'Question Time'.

For all her aggressive style of writing and trenchant habits of speech, Rosalind Miles has very little to say which is new; but that is her special value in this discussion. From the ganglion of her prejudices and assumptions can be drawn all the fibres of misconception, untruth and intolerance which have come to comprise the body of feminist axioms and the articles of feminist faith in the last quarter of a century. On the issues of domestic violence and of rape, for instance, her utterances are indistinguishable from those of Sandra Horley, Director of the Chiswick Family Rescue (formerly Chiswick Women's Aid). Miles believes (and I shall have a lot more to say about this later) that all women are held in subjection by all men who will employ the brutalities of wife-battering and of rape to express their power and to have their way. Rosalind Miles's views upon pornography and the insult to all women which is supposed to be delivered by the appearance of half-naked girls on tabloid Page Threes are the same as those expressed by Clare Short MP. Miles has said that women should not be embarrassed to line up with Mary Whitehouse in demanding the censorship of those images.

Permed, powdered and lipsticked as she appears before the cameras, the attitudes she expresses towards feminine dress and decoration are no different from the beliefs espoused by feminist writers over twenty years – from Robin Morgan's *Sisterhood is Powerful* and Susan Brownmiller's *Femininity* to Naomi Wolfe's *The Beauty Myth* – that a male culture requires women to torture and degrade themselves in uncomfortable attire and a mask of cosmetics (at the same time, Miles and others like her constantly affirm that women dress to please themselves and other women).

Every fusty cliché in the established canon of feminist

orthodoxy gets an outing in her writings and sayings. When, for instance, she was interviewed by Anne Kelleher on BBC 2's 'Fighting Talk', she repeated many of the standard lines of the feminist sisterhood, including that ancient and hoary saw about a woman without a man being like a fish without a bicycle. She also said that many women had found that it was essential to the development of their feminism to recognise that their true enemy is not an ideological 'ism' but is, in fact, the individual man in their lives. Those women, she said, had had to come to terms with the old slogan that 'The personal is political'.

Anne Kelleher and Dr Miles agreed that their own husbands were not included in the lists of the enemy. They agreed that the political issue before them was not expressed in the quality of their own personal lives. They agreed, therefore, that they were discussing the misfortunes of other women and the qualities of men in general.

The generality of men is Rosalind Miles's particular speciality and she approaches her subject with a tangible confidence that her generalisations will not be doubted or questioned. Only one who regarded herself as being immune to sceptical questioning could commit a sentence to print which says that more men consult their doctors about impotence than any other ailment.

Think about it. Can it *possibly* be true? If you are a man, think of yourself and the men who are your closest friends. If you are a woman, think of the men you have known most intimately. How many of them have gone to the doctor to discuss their impotence? How many of them have gone more frequently to the doctor for that reason rather than to beg for relief from colds, bunions or bouts of flu? Don't say that you wouldn't know because men would keep it secret. Miles is telling us, in effect, that men consult their doctors about impotence regularly, routinely, as often as women go for a

26

cervical smear-test. A national phenomenon on that scale could not be a secret.

If you think there is even the dimmest glimmer of a possibility that Rosalind Miles might be telling the truth, I urge you to put the question to your own General Practitioner. I asked mine. This is what he said.

> DOCTOR: 'That's the most extraordinary statement. It belies reality. I am consulted on impotence, I would say, once in every year or two. Consultations on disorders in the upper respiratory tract run at . . .'
>
> LYNDON: 'A hundred and fifty a week, I'd guess.'
>
> DOCTOR: 'Well, possibly, some weeks . . . Consultations on impotence are really extremely rare because most people simply accept the condition as part of the ageing process — not something which medical science can put right.'

So Rosalind Miles's line appears, inexcusably, to be wholly inaccurate. There is not a molecule of truth in it. It is wrong in fact and it would even be thoroughly false if it were being used in metaphorical senses: which it was not. To view this 'mistake' most benignly, it has to be counted as moronic fancy carelessly committed to print without a thought for reason and probability. To view it less kindly, it can be counted a stinking lie.

You may think that I am getting excited on this point because the subject is the feebleness and failure of the phallus and, as is well known, men are particularly and pathetically sensitive on that issue.

If that's what you're thinking, you should go and boil your head to clear your thoughts. One of the reasons why Rosalind Miles felt free to commit that ridiculous line to print was that she knew no man would invite the derision which would result from any challenge. It's not the size and potency of the organ which is in question: it is the scale and quality of the dishonesty which counts.

Why did she say it? How is it possible that a writer capable of composing such a demonstrably false and malignant line should be accorded the respect of the country's critical establishment and, indeed, be conferred academic respectability and a salary from the public purse? (The dust-jacket of her book tells us that Rosalind Miles 'founded the Centre for Women's Studies at Coventry Polytechnic' and that 'in 1990 she was appointed a Fellow of the Royal Society of Arts'.)

The answers to those questions must inhere, I want to argue, in the subject itself. Rosalind Miles felt free to commit that sentence to print because it would not have crossed her mind that anybody might question it. The general experience of the last twenty years (and, presumably, Dr Miles's own experience as she has advanced to the salons of the Royal Society of Arts and the panels of broadcasting pundits) would have cemented in her mind a doubtless confidence in her own rectitude.

How could she be wrong on any point when all her attitudes, beliefs and presumptions were confirmed in the broader society? She knew, as by automatic instinct, what every woman writing in public and speaking in private had come to know – that, on the subject of men and their inadequacies, their failings, their evils and their wrongdoings, any assertion might be made without fear of argument.

My sceptical reader may feel, again, that a big deal is being made out of a small slip. Let's, then, put our minds to a monstrous lie of Dr Miles's – a lie which is, in fact, the intellectual raison d'être of her book and is one of the essential tenets of modern feminism. It is one of the bigger lies of the century, a real ranker. It deserves a place in the

horror-show of twentieth-century totalitarianisms along-
side the lie that all Jews were in league with the Reds to
poison and to rob Aryan peoples. Rosalind Miles did not
invent her lie. She is merely a willing agent for its transmission.

She says, in so many words, that violence can be explained
if we can explain the male and vice versa.

Let's take those sentiments in our hands and pull them
around. Let's try to tear from them the stuff of casuistry and
intolerance with which they are made – a form of violence
which seems to this man to be urgently needed and wholly
justified in self-defence.

First of all, let's fiddle with the terms and do that switch-
trick again. How do the sentiments of Rosalind Miles appear
if you substitute another evil, say, usury, for the crime of
violence and another general group, say, Jews, for men? This
is what you get.

> To explain usury is to explain the Jew. The reverse is
> also true . . .

and

> The truth about usury is that Jewishness itself
> provides the key . . . As the linking thread between
> usurers is that they are Jews then it is to Jewishness
> itself that we must look for the answer to its origins
> and for any hope of its remedy.

If that passage had appeared in print in any of the developed
countries of the world having been written by an academic
who is paid from public funds and who is a member of one of
that country's leading and most respected cultural institutions, pandemonium would result. She would be booted out
of tenure at her college and her resignation would be
demanded at the Royal Society. Only the most rabid of
fascist fanatics would compose that thought in print; and

only the most marginal of one-man band publishers would disseminate it.

The reason why those sentiments would not be allowed ought not to need expression; but I have to set it down so that I can carry it back to the original terms of Rosalind Miles's propositions.

The reason we would not say that Jewishness equals usury and vice versa is not, principally, because we may feel tender to the memories of those millions of Jews who suffered and died when the German nation came to believe in the truth of that declaration and others like it. The reason we would not say it is because we know that it is not true. It cannot be true that all Jews are usurers because, in logic and in truth, there are bound to be multitudes who are not. Even if the Jew in the top flat of your building *is* a usurer, you are not entitled to presume that the other Jew whom you see every morning at the bus stop is also a usurer. Even if the Jew in the top flat has exacted interest from you to the last farthing of your fortune, you may not go further than to say 'In my experience, a usurer may be a Jew', allowing for the varieties which dictate that a usurer may not be a Jew and that a Jew may be anything. You may not presume, bien entendue, that all usurers are Jews or that all Jews are usurers. Everybody in the West with a grain of reason or a particle of understanding in their head has agreed upon this principle, as far as it applies to the Jews, since the gates of Belsen were pushed open, laying bare the bones of the victims of that genus of casuistry.

For identical reasons, we may not say that black people are less intelligent than white people: it *cannot* be true. If there is only one black person on earth who is more intelligent than one white person, the statement that blacks are less intelligent than whites fails. Any survey or investigation which reports that blacks are *on average* less

30

intelligent than whites would, rightly, be subjected to
ferocious scrutiny and criticism and its terms of measure-
ment would be subjected to detailed examination for signs of
prejudice. We would suppose that the terms of the investigation had been framed to produce a desired result. We
recognise that, if we say white people are more intelligent
than blacks, we make it impossible for the black who is more
intelligent than another white to express that intelligence:
we confine him, unjustly, with bars of prejudice. Base
prejudice of that order is admissible only among sots and
half-wits who are not normally admitted as Fellows of the
Royal Society of Arts.

Now let's imagine that Dr Miles were a Roger rather than
a Rosalind and that he were a lecturer in Social Psychology
at Warwick University rather than being the founder of the
Centre for Women's Studies at Coventry Polytechnic. Let's
suppose that Dr Roger had written:

> To explain deception is to explain the female. The
> reverse is also true . . .

and that he had gone on to say:

> The truth about female deceit is that femaleness itself
> provides the key . . . As the linking thread between
> deceivers is that they are female then it is to
> femininity itself that we must look for the answer to
> its origins and for any hope of its remedy.

Kiss goodbye to your campus ass, Dr Roger (I trust you don't
really exist). Those charming days in the groves of academe
just ended for ever, brother. Take this broom and go and
sweep the streets for penance and never lift your eyes again
to an abstract thought or an ermine collar.

Nobody who draws his living from academic work in the
West would dare – even if he believed it – to commit such a
heresy to print. The notion that women might share an

31

inbuilt evil, because they are female, is so far from the established orthodoxies of thought and expression in our time that it is, truly, unthinkable. It would offend so radically against the feminist articles of faith that it would be, in every sense, unpublishable. Dr Roger would know better than to risk his ass.

He would also understand, we may hope, that the notion offends against the standing orders of his trade because it would be demonstrably insupportable. Anybody who has progressed in the study of the liberal humanities beyond Stage One SAT's would know better than to advance the proposition that all deceivers are female and all females are deceivers: like all other totalitarian lies, it is a base offence against the rules of reason; it cannot be true.

Those rules, evidently, do not apply to Dr Rosalind. She obviously feels free to bundle together those principles like a faggot and lob them into the flames of the Reichstag fire. Her stipend, if she has one, will not be withdrawn. The invitations to the studios will continue to arrive. She knows that her place is unassailable.

Here comes an assault.

It cannot be true to say, as she does, that to explain violence is to explain the male. It cannot be true to say, as she does, that the reverse also applies any more than it can be true to say that usury explains the Jew and the Jew explains usury. The proposition is logically indefensible in each of its parts. Violence is not exclusive to men; nor is it common to all men; nor is it the sole connective characteristic of masculinity. According to the rules and principles by which degrees, doctorates and fellowships are supposed to be awarded, the totalitarian vulgarities of Rosalind Miles's methods and styles of assertion ought to have made her persona non grata in the academic world. Instead of which, she was given a Centre all her own.

32

We can make more of a mess out of Rosalind Miles's lines of cant if we take them outside the cerebral theatre of abstract argument and measure them against recorded realities in the world.

It needs to be said, in the first place, that ours is not a very violent society, even by comparison with other similar countries. Crimes of violence such as assault are committed more often in Britain today than they were thirty years ago but they occur less often in Britain than in Germany or Switzerland – countries where poverty, homelessness, unemployment and racial tensions are markedly less widespread than in our own.

By comparison with the United States, Great Britain is a remarkably pacific society. The marks of this comparison are stunning. A glimpse of them can be drawn from the murder statistics.

We all share an uneasy sense that murders are being committed more frequently in Britain and that we are at greater risk than we used to be of a senseless attack which might kill us. We are mistaken. The incidence of murder has remained constant and steady for about twenty years, numbering some 600 victims a year in England and Wales. This total is smaller than the number of murders committed every year in Los Angeles alone. A more graphic comparison can be made between the most violent corners of British and American society, between Northern Ireland and New York.

The present troubles in Northern Ireland have lasted twenty-three years. Throughout that period, the territory has been extensively garrisoned and has been regulated by a form of martial law: Northern Ireland has been a society self-evidently at war with itself and, during those two decades, the exploits of terrorists have occupied the attentions of the whole world, making a political and social problem which is universally agreed to be one of the most grievous and intractable anywhere.

In the first twenty years of the troubles in Northern Ireland, some 2,500 people were murdered. This figure includes all the victims of terrorist atrocity and all the members of the British Army and of the security services who have been killed.

In New York City, some 20,000 people were murdered in the Eighties. In that single city, the average number of murders for every year of that decade approached the total number of people murdered in Northern Ireland in two decades of war.

It is, therefore, unreasonable to claim – as Rosalind Miles claims throughout *The Rites of Man* and in many of her public declarations – that violence is a rising tide and that no one is safe and no one is free. That, she says, is the truth of our world. I maintain the opposite. Most British adults will die without having experienced a single episode of violence in their adult lives, neither as victims nor as perpetrators. The same is true, even given the frightening incidence of violence in American cities, of citizens of the United States.

Am I trying to argue that crimes of violence do not happen in Great Britain? I am not. Am I trying to deny that these crimes are mostly committed by males? I am not.

I am trying to draw elementary distinctions. And I want to show that, in ignoring those distinctions, Rosalind Miles and the feminist orthodoxy for which she speaks are employing totalitarian habits of mind with pernicious results.

There is, plainly, a problem of violence in Britain. It is evident in every city centre when the clubs and the pubs tip out and, again, on Saturday afternoon when the local football club plays at home and the city receives the bands of supporters who have travelled with the visiting team.

Those fighting drunks and those foul-mouthed chanting thugs are all male and they are a menace. It is very important to emphasise that they are chiefly a menace to each other and to themselves. It is also an elementary observation to say that they are nearly all young.

Of the crimes of violence which occur in Britain, nearly all are committed by *and upon* males who are between the ages of fifteen and twenty-five. The incidence of violence between and among young men tails away dramatically after the age of twenty and declines to near zero among men over the age of thirty.

Violence among young men is a frightful scene and a horrible problem. It would be better for them and better for the rest of us if they could find some less aggressive forms of demonstration for their tribal loyalties and some less gory rites of passage from childhood to adulthood. But there it is — a problem which we must all address as citizens and one which, praise be, does not pose an immediate threat to our own security and safety in the way which, for instance, the menace of traffic accidents applies equally to all of us.

Rosalind Miles and the feminist orthodoxy for which she speaks would not have us see the issue in this light. She wants us to see the question in terms which divide men and women and cast them into disconnected and eternally opposing armed camps. Let's look again at her specific terms. She says that the connection between violent offenders is the fact that they are male; and she goes on to say that the explanation for the origins of violence may be found in the nature of masculinity itself.

Two lines of casuistry can be extracted from those sentiments. The first is the underlying assumption that all offences of violence are committed by men. The second and consequential assumption is that violence, being unique to men, must be an element in the genetic coding of masculinity, a feature of masculine physiology which can be identified like testosterone.

The reader may recognise some familiar tones here: the

idea that a social evil is a physiological constituent of a group of people in the connective tissue of totalitarianism in many of its guises, religious and political. Dr Goebbels cast it upon the airwaves with his thoughts about the chemical composition of Semitic evil.

Is it true that all offences of violence are committed by men? Obviously, it is not true. Even if we confine an investigation merely to the crimes of violence which are officially recognised and recorded, we see that some women attack, injure and destroy their fellow humans.

In Great Britain, for every woman who murders her husband or lover some three men murder their wives or lovers. Neither group is very large. Roughly speaking, twenty men are murdered by their women every year. About sixty women are murdered by their men. Feminist lobbyists such as the QC Helena Kennedy have insistently tried to argue that there is a vital qualitative difference between the murder of women by men and the murder of men by women – a difference which ought to place those women murderers in a different dimension of responsibility and blame from the murdering men. That is, I believe, their way of saying that those murders are not real.

Since some women really do commit murder, it cannot be argued that the linking factor between violent offenders is their masculinity. Whatever their motives, whatever their special or shared circumstances, those women murderers rupture that line of cant. The only reasonable deduction which can be drawn from the murder statistics is that, of the very few murders which are committed in Britain, many more are committed by men than by women and it seems reasonable to guess that something dreadful must have occurred in the lives of those individuals. Broader inferences on the essential qualities and nature of gender are simply insupportable.

The evident facts speak against those inferences if you

look further into the recorded figures and then cast your eyes around the society in which we live. It becomes apparent that some forms of violence which are, in fact, more common to women than to men are simply not counted as violence in the terms which apply to men. Those acts of violence are viewed and treated as if they are not real.

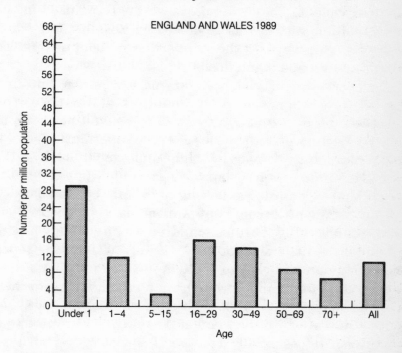

Take homicide again. If you look at the graphs issued by the Home Office in the annual crime figures, you will see that the largest group of victims of murder is composed of babies. Murder victims under the age of one year outnumber any other group in our society – even among the reckless and fist-happy tribes of adolescent males. Most of those babies are murdered by their mothers. Many of them are beaten to death. The crime is not counted as murder. It exists in the separate category of infanticide. The perpetrators are

37

accorded special treatment in the courts and are most unlikely to be sentenced to any long term of detention (I am not saying that the courts ought to treat them unsympathetically nor that they should necessarily be banged up in chokey: I am simply drawing more distinctions).

By any measure, the actions of those women must be counted violent. They are not, however, recognised in the canons of feminist law as advanced by Rosalind Miles and every other purveyor of the standard cant about men which fills our newspapers and floods across the airwaves.

Another form of violence, far more common but universally ignored, is visible all around us, all the time. You can see it on every bus, in every doctor's waiting-room, at every school-gate, in the aisles of every supermarket; and it is predominantly female in origin and execution. It is the casual administration of slaps, whacks and thumps by adults on children. The routine belting of infants by exasperated adults draws little comment among us and, despite the wailing and crying of bruised children which sounds through all our days, little disapprobation. Since women are much more commonly in charge of children in public places than men, we see many more women than men laying into their kids; but we do not see those beltings as acts of violence. Our sympathies are with the women. We take it for granted that being a parent, especially a mother, is such a trying business that it cannot be surprising to see many mothers – especially the ignorant, the uneducated and the unrefined – hammering their nippers.

Why has Rosalind Miles chosen to ignore these categories and types of female violence? Why do they not register in her mind nor make their way into her writing? Why do feminists of all persuasions and shades of opinion want to insist that men share universal characteristics of behaviour and habits of thought? Why are they so unwilling to acknowledge

38

similarities between men and women and differences between men?

The answer I must give is that the incubus of feminist casuistry demands that all men must be thought to be identical. At the heart of the incubus, as in the heart of all forms of totalitarian prejudice, is the insistence that *they are all the same* – Jews, Muslims, blacks, Scots – and men. For all its decorations of scholarship, its titles, its fellowships and its study centres, the philosophical drive of modern feminism comes down to a barbarous and totalitarian simplicity: men are all the same and, in their very masculinity, they share an inherent evil.

I first tried to sketch a picture of this incubus, giving some indication of its scale and influence, in a big article published by the *Sunday Times Magazine* in December 1990. Let me reproduce here the specimens of routine and habitual expression of prejudice towards men which I had un-systematically collected from 1989–1990 while I was work-ing on the preparation of that article.

> GERMAINE GREER: 'It always amazes me that women don't understand how much men hate them'. This line of Greer's dates from the early Seventies. I picked it up again when it was published with approval in a television listings' column in the *Independent* in the spring of 1990.

Ask yourself: does Greer mean that all men hate all women all the time? does she mean that men *only* hate women and do not love them? or does she mean that individual men may love individual women but, regardless, all men hate women? Your choice.

> A LAPEL BADGE: 'The more men I meet, the more I like my dog.' I saw this in a hotel dime-store in New York in June 1990.

Imagine what might happen to a producer of novelties who marketed a badge saying 'The more women I meet the more I like my dog' or even 'The more dogs I meet the more I like my woman'.

ANNA RAEBURN, counsellor: 'I regard men as a pleasant pastime but no more dependable than the British weather.' Raeburn delivered herself of this line in the winter of 1990 in a television discussion programme chaired by Mike Scott to mark the twentieth anniversary of the introduction of the contraceptive pill for women.

Put these words in the mouth of a man on television speaking about women: hear the hisses from the studio audience.

SALLY O'SULLIVAN, editor of women's magazines, who said she 'prefers working with women having found men on newspapers "real old back-stabbing chatterboxes" '. These words were printed in a trade paper when Sally O'Sullivan was appointed editor of *Harper's* magazine. She is now editor of *Good House-keeping*.

Put those words in the mouth of a male editor speaking about women. Imagine how long he would keep his job.

JANE FONDA: 'I still believe that women are the superior sex.' This line came from a profile of Fonda published by the colour magazine of the *Los Angeles Times* in the autumn of 1989.

If she thinks that there is or can be a 'superior sex', it must follow that there can be superior races and nationalities, superior lines of genealogy, superior castes and classes. Anybody who says that there can be such a thing as a

40

superior sex must either not know or must be rejecting the post-Enlightenment and revolutionary assumptions of Western civilisation about the equality of all individuals and their essential freedoms. We have to assume that the meaning and purpose of the French and American Revolutions have slipped past Jane Fonda.

> JULIE BURCHILL writing in *Time Out* in the autumn of 1989: 'A good part – and definitely the most fun part – of being a feminist is about frightening men. American and Australian feminists have always known this, and absorbed it cheerfully into their act; one thinks of Shere Hite julienning men on phone-in shows, or Dale Spender telling us that a good feminist is rude to a man at least three times a day ON PRINCIPLE. Of course, there's a lot more to feminism ... but scaring the shit out of the scumbags is an amusing and necessary part because, sadly, a good many men still respect nothing but strength.'

Try substituting the word 'Nazi' for 'feminist' and 'Jew' for 'man'. Bring a strong stomach to the exercise.

> JANET DALEY, columnist, at the time, for the *Independent*, writing in 1990: 'The standard Western adult male is rendered incapable of being comfortable with emotional expression ... being quite incapable of understanding what it is like to be someone else.'

'The standard male'? Am I he? Is he my brother? Is any one of my colleagues and friends a standard male? If there is a 'standard male', may I be introduced to him; and, at the same time, may I also meet his sister, the 'standard female' who finds it so easy to imagine what it is like to be me?

JONATHAN MILLER, speaking to *The Times* in a profile published in 1990: 'Men don't get on well with each other, they don't have standards of intimacy, so they exchange jokes.'

Oh, don't I and do I? Don't you and do you? Thanks a billion – or two – Dr Miller.

CAROLINE JENKINS, a correspondent writing on the Letters' page of the *Radio Times*, in 1990, following a television programme about divorced or separated fathers who have trouble seeing their children: 'Mothers bring children into the world and mothers bring them up. Fathers mostly sit about on their behinds watching the television while mothers feed the kids, bath the kids, play with the kids, tell the kids bedtime stories and generally wear themselves out. Most fathers can't be bothered to spend more than half an hour with their kids until they have grown up or until their exhausted wives see the light and divorce them.'

I think I may strangle this woman. Germaine Greer will say that's because I hate women. It is not true. I hate what *this* woman says; and I don't harbour entirely friendly feelings, I will admit, towards Dr Greer for her sayings.

SARAH KENT, art critic of *Time Out* writing in 1990 about an exhibition in London of the works of Yoko Ono: 'I see [Yoko] Ono's approach as a strategy for survival in a deeply sexist era. Her observations, frequently couched as humour, hit home with deadly accuracy. "I wonder why men can get serious at all," she wrote ... "They have this delicate long thing hanging outside their bodies which goes up and down by its own will ... Humour is probably something the male of the species discovered through his own anatomy." '

'Labial lips and a clitoris are the funniest things on earth,' quoth the fashionable artist, soon to meet his maker.

ERICA JONG speaking through a character in the novel *Any Woman's Blues*, published 1990, which she declared to be largely autobiographical: 'Maleness is wonderful, really, isn't it, honey? Perfect denial of reality.'

May I say 'Femaleness is wonderful: perfect denial of reality'? I may not. As it happens, I don't want to say it, but that's not the point.

My sceptical reader may remain unconvinced. You may feel that the specimens I have given do not amount to a genuine phenomenon, that the items of spite or of evil intolerance which I have listed do not make an incubus. You may think that my Hartlepool experience is slight, that Rosalind Miles is a nobody, that the reproduction of passages from last year's magazine article merely treads on beaten ground.

I don't know how much further to go in trying to answer those uncertainties. I am eager to move on to the consideration of questions such as: Why is this incubus around us? Where did it come from? And are we going to have to live with it for the rest of our lives? But if you won't agree that the evidence I have given and the evidence of your own eyes and ears confirms the presence of this unwholesome thing, then we're a bit stuck on the first lap. Let me try to answer those uncertainties by listing here a few further examples which have come my way during the months of 1991 when I have been working on this book. The first batch got lodged on the computer's memory in the first two weeks of that year,

43

during which something happened which extended the licence of derision, hatred and contempt towards men.

> JANE MCLOUGHLIN, author of *The Demographic Revolution*: 'We'll wear you [men] like alligator handbags' – speaking on the BBC TV programme 'Behind the Headlines', 9 January 1991.

So men are reptiles?

> 'War is menstrual envy' – demonstrators' placard in Whitehall, seen on 11 January 1991.

Oh, is *that* what it is? The scales drop from my eyes at last.

> JOY MELVILLE: 'According to one recent poll, far more women than men are opposed to military action in the Gulf. Where, then, is the passion against men and their military gains . . . ?' *The Times*, 16 January 1991.

So if you're against the war you've got to be against men because men=violence=war . . . but then you know that syllogism.

Shall we go on? Have you had enough? You could start your own collection. The items I have recorded here are no more than a small selection of the specimens I have collected. I've got a file full of them in the bottom drawer of a filing-cabinet. You don't need to see them all, do you? Let me just go and pull out the top three, the most recent I have filed.

In the 1991 summer/autumn issue of the British style magazine *Arena*, an article was published entitled 'The Facts About Female Bonding' by Kimberley Leston. She wrote:

Unlike men, women do not need to drink in order to bond. To the outsider female bonding is a seemingly instantaneous business, a phenomenon that is as natural and fluid to women as it is forced and effortful to men; which makes it all the more mysterious and enviable to men who have to tread the fine line between consciousness and oblivion before they can achieve even the most rudimentary state of bonding.

You may not know that *Arena* is a magazine of high fashion. Its pages express the thoughts and attitudes of style-makers. It exists and it succeeds because it offers clues, signposts and images to those who are anxious to know what is being worn and thought by fashionable people – what they are doing, where they are going and how they spend their money. Of one thing, therefore, we may be sure: an article in *Arena* – as in any other publication – may be muddle-headed, poorly argued, falsely construed, but it will not be square; the attitudes it expresses are likely to be bang on the button of prevailing beliefs in fashionable metropolitan groups. The opinions and prejudices of Kimberley Leston may not be shared by the editors of *Arena*, but we may be confident that those opinions are common in the society in which Kimberley Leston moves. Otherwise, she wouldn't have been asked to write and her article would not have been published.

We don't need, do we, to separate the grains of idiocy in that specimen of prejudice? Let's just nail it to the totem and leave it there for posterity. I only want to remark, in passing, that Sister Kimberley has come a long way from the ladies who helped to give birth to the prejudices she now feels free to air. I remember that, in the early Seventies at Laurieston Hall, an experimental commune in the Border counties where young revolutionaries lived together to break the conventions of nuclear family life, the women felt the need to find 'new forms of bonding'.

Men, those Laurieston sisters said, were the inheritors of multiple forms of bonding, from the pub to the bowls' club, from the allotment to the commuter train, from the Long Room at Lord's to the dining-table in the Mess. Men had uniforms, jokes, songs and rituals. Women, they reckoned, had no equivalent variety of bonding opportunities other than the communal washing-machine and the knitting circle. Something must be done, they declared, to make up for this cultural deficiency which was an aspect of women's oppression.

Twenty years later, what have you got? 'To the outsider female bonding is a seemingly instantaneous business, a phenomenon that is as natural and fluid to women as it is forced and effortful to men.'

Sweet, eh?

Here's the next one. This comes from a review published in the *London Review of Books*, 15 August 1991. The article is entitled 'Looking for the loo'. It is a review by Dr Mary Beard, who teaches ancient history at Cambridge and is a Fellow of Newnham College, of a book called *You Just Don't Understand: Women and Men in Conversation*, by Deborah Tannen.

Dr Beard condensed Deborah Tannen's argument as follows:

> Men, she argues, use conversation as a means of establishing status; they use it to get and keep attention; they use it to exhibit their own knowledge and skill – 'holding centre stage through verbal performance such as storytelling, joking, or imparting information'. Women, by contrast, use talk as a means of establishing intimacy, connection and

46

rapport; they use it not as a mechanism of domination, but as a part of a 'negotiation for closeness, in which people try to seek and give confirmation and support and to reach consensus'. If this is right, it can be no surprise that women working in male institutions feel a sense of not belonging: they can never quite be one of the lads, because in the last resort they do not talk the lads' language.

You may not know that, within a small society, the *London Review of Books* is as much a style-maker as *Arena*. Among academics who work in the liberal humanities and in London's literary establishment of reviewers, publishers and editors, the *London Review of Books* is an essential tool of navigation, charting the stars of present achievement and the black holes of critical failure. The *London Review of Books* is, then, genuinely influential – the people it influences themselves influence a broader society.

Do you find yourself agreeing with any or all of the presumptions in the passage I have quoted? Is it true, in your experience, that men and women speak different languages when they are side by side in the same institutions? Is it correct, in your experience, to call those institutions 'male'?

That passage sure as hell doesn't tally with my experience. I have found the opposite of the patterns Deborah Tannen observes and Mary Beard endorses. What strikes me most forcibly about the emergence of women in large numbers in all walks of life in the last twenty-five years is not the very great difference that they have effected in the internal workings and external qualities of those institutions but the extent to which those functions and qualities have remained exactly the same.

Having frequently retained or consulted women doctors or lawyers, estate agents, literary agents or business advisers, having had regular and constant dealings with women educators and administrators, having met, done business with or interviewed hundreds of women in business or politics, having frequently worked with and for women as colleagues, what impresses me most vividly is not the qualitative differences in performance or attitude between men and women in those professions but the extent to which those elements are indistinguishable.

The performances of women in government are immensely revealing in this regard. When women ministers speak on behalf of governments or when women officials are appointed to deliver explanations of policy, I do not detect *any* differences in language or in an order of priorities between those women and their male counterparts. The appearances of the State Department's woman representative at daily press conferences during the Gulf War was a powerful instance; what differences were visible or audible between her performances and those which might have been expected from a man? None that I could see. When women presenters read the news or interview politicians, I do not see obvious differences, nor even subtle differences, between their work and the work of the men beside them.

There is an automatic feminist answer to this line of observation: they say that women are compelled to adopt male mannerisms in male institutions. That is why, they say, Margaret Thatcher's performance as Prime Minister was exaggeratedly bellicose, authoritarian and uncompromising: to succeed in a male preserve, she had to become more of a man than the men.

That strikes me as being one of the more pustulent lines of piss in the crock of cant which is modern feminism. It is so unintelligent and insensitive, so feeble as an account of the origins and purposes of political institutions, that we wouldn't, in any time other than our own, give it the time of

48

day if it emerged from the drooling mouth of a drunk at a bar. Now we find it underpinning the arguments of a Fellow of Newnham College and rehearsed in the pages of a journal which is broadly admired among educated people throughout the West.

It is such a widely held presumption among the educated classes that it has to be answered with elementary simplicities.

Political, social and commercial institutions in a modern society come into being and take their shape, character and purpose in response to the contemporary needs of that society. The social and economic forces which shape them are impersonal, genderless, neutral.

The office of Prime Minister did not come into being and was not ordained to be male because that's the way men like it any more than the office of chief inspector of Eastern Counties' buses is a preserve of patriarchy. Each office took its origin in the external circumstances of the day in which it was created. Those external circumstances did not, at the time, include women as candidates for office. Their exclusion was incidental to those circumstances, not intrinsic to the social, political or commercial demands which the offices answered. When that incidental dimension of external circumstances changed – for reasons which I explore at length in later chapters – and women emerged as candidates for office, the institutions remained the same.

I see this most clearly in my own business and in my interests in education – the media and education being two sectors of business life and of public service which have been most extensively penetrated by women in the last twenty-five years.

I have been working as a professional journalist for twenty-two years. The first piece of work I was ever employed to write was commissioned by a woman editor.

This book, my present work, was originally commissioned by women. I haven't done a count of heads but I would reckon that the women I have worked with or for in the last twenty-two years must be roughly equal to the number of men who have given me work or acted as colleagues in those years. Maybe I'm exaggerating a touch: let's call it seven men for every five women.

The only difference I can record or remember between the experiences of those years as they might divide between men and women has been the possibility – as has happened in a handful of instances – that a sexual relationship might develop between me and the woman I was working with. That explosive element of chance has made some difference to my fortunes but not much, I feel. Perhaps I have been given work by a few women who wanted to advance a personal connection. I may have been refused some work by women who did not relish the closer connection I fancied. Perhaps I have been denied work by women who were offended by my unwillingness to get into bed with them or by some who were not pleased by my behaviour when we got there or afterwards.

In any event, the difference doesn't amount to much: a similar dimension of personal complication has affected my relations with some male employers and colleagues. A few of the editors who have employed me have numbered among my best men friends. When our friendships have been particularly close and going well, I may have had more work from them than at other times; when we have fallen out over a personal disagreement or crisis, the flow of work commissioned from them has dried up. So it goes.

In their purely professional capacities, in the demands of their work and in the ways they executed their responsibilities, the men and women I have worked with have been indistinguishable from each other and interchangeable.

50

Good, sensitive and imaginative editors have not all been female; undependable, idle, time-serving and uninventive editors have not all been male.

Within the terms of language and the styles of speech employed by these men and women there has been no difference defined by or explained by their gender. The language of deadlines, headlines, word-counts, page make-ups and print-runs is, as it must be, equally shared by the men and women who are practitioners of that business. The language is neuter (rather than being a 'genderlect' as the Mses Beard and Tannen would say) because it emerges from and is universal to the demands of the business. Within the more personal minutiae of the business of journalism – the definitions of subject, the listing of questions, the arrangement of paragraphs, the syntax of sentences – I cannot say that I have ever been aware of constant and consistent differences between the practices of the men and women I have worked with. A subject is interesting and worthwhile or it is not; a question is telling and revealing or it is not; a paragraph or sentence makes sense or it does not. Occasionally, a woman editor has instructed me to ask a question or to write a paragraph because, she says, 'this is a woman's question' or 'women will want to know'. I have always despised those lines just as I have contempt for the male editors who presume that some subjects – sport, business, cars – cannot be framed and conveyed to engage the interests of women readers. The presumptions display the limits of the editors' own intelligence and professional skill rather than the inherent qualities of a subject or the natural and unalterable preferences and tastes of readers. There is, as great old hacks tend to say, no such thing as a limited subject; only limited journalists.

Turning to the behaviour of men and women in meetings and in conversation, I have not found the differences between the performances of men and women which Beard/ Tannen relate. I do not believe they can be squared with visible realities. I believe, as with every other example of feminist cant in this chapter, as with every other constituent of the incubus which I have been trying to describe, that the distinctions they are drawing are fictional inventions for the pernicious purpose of dividing men and women into opposing groups, classes and genetic compositions.

When I go to an editorial meeting or to a legal conference, to a gathering of school governors in my county or to meetings of governors and staff at the primary school where I am a parent governor, I do not see the distinctions which Beard and Tannen advance. Some women are reticent or silent in these meetings. So are some of the men. Some women use the occasions as vehicles for ego-display, 'holding centre stage through verbal performance'; and so do some men. Some men are, plainly, trying to 'establish intimacy, connection and rapport' with others in those meetings; some women are going the same way. Sometimes, the women and men who have been standing up on their hind legs holding centre stage will drop that performance and turn to the creation of intimacy with the ones who are sitting beside them (this is often as much a nuisance of distraction from the business on the agenda as the stage-storming which has preceded it).

Some of the participants in these meetings make sense to the others; some don't. Some are capable of speaking coherently about the subject which has been agreed to be under consideration; some aren't. The abilities and the qualities of those participants cannot be regulated or recognised by the outline of their genitals. Nor is it true that the specific terms and words employed by the participants differ between men and women. They speak the same language.

The jerking feminist knee goes for this observation in the

nuts by declaring that shared language to be the language of a male institution – 'the lads' language', as Dr Beard says. The knee misses the nuts. The institution is not male; the language is not male. The institution and its functions, the language of its agenda and the minutiae of its business are neutral, genderless, impersonal.

That's why *everybody* working in those institutions feels 'a sense of not belonging'. I can say that I loved the little primary school down the lane when my son was enrolled there; but I felt less than easy at meetings of the governors and still less sure of myself, my motives and my place when packets of instructions and regulations came in the post from the Secretary of State. Institutions require from every individual who enters their service a degree of surrender, release or elimination of ego and self. That's why they are called institutions. The individual submits personal needs to the agreed purposes and benefits of the corporate body. Institutions, by their very existence, function collectively, according to regulated authority and by the agreement of their members.

Individuals – men or women – who identify themselves wholly and unreservedly with institutions are known as fruit-cakes. The teacher who has no life outside the school, the soldier whose entire personality has been drilled in the ranks, the banker who dies of ego extinction when his fourteen-hour days at his desk must cease – these people are all regarded as being a few marbles short of a full bag. Something is missing from them if their entire sense of belonging in the world is vested in the life of an institution.

Anybody who assumes that men discover and enjoy in institutions a comprehensive sense of belonging which women lack has not been listening to men or must wilfully be ignoring realities for the sake of a fictitious account. If there is one outstanding common theme among and between the complaints which modern men have expressed for the last three hundred years, it is a sense of 'not belonging' in the institutions of the modern state – from church to army, from government to bank, from marriage to prison. Great God Almighty, this is the very essence of the alienations which men have described from Goldsmith and Fielding and Gray and Shelley to Thoreau and Emerson, Mailer and Bob Dylan. What the hell else have they and we been carrying on about?

Dr Beard lives and works in one of those institutions where men can most frequently be heard complaining of a sense of 'not belonging'. When I was an undergraduate at Cambridge, at a time when men outnumbered women by, it was said, thirteen to one, young men could be found in their rooms at any time of day or night slumped in a paralysis of despair because, they felt, they did not belong. I was, myself, one of those grieving and whimpering depressives. One of the main reasons why we felt so hopelessly alienated was the absence of women which was – anybody who was there will agree – top of the list of our complaints about that institution. The boys who are Cambridge undergraduates today, when more or less equal numbers of girls are admitted, have been spared that particular dimension of discomforting alienation; and I am glad for them. But I will bet a pound to a penny that they are still, in droves and thousands, in misery night and day with a sense of not belonging. Only an observer with one ear and one eye closed would be unaware of that misery; or capable of the presumption that the language of lads, if there is such a thing, conveys only a sense of the belonging of those lads in institutions rather than a sense of displacement, compromise and the reduction or elimination of self.

Are you with me? Are we getting anywhere? I can go on listing examples of spoken or written prejudice about men, dubious in their reasoning or faulty in their evidence, for another 20,000 words. I can take them apart in the way I have attacked foregoing examples; but we may have carried this approach as far as it will go.

My purpose in this chapter has been to try to show that an incubus is in the air all around us, that it has the sanction and approval of powerful makers of fashion in attitude and belief. We can see, I hope, that it finds expression in the mouths of world-famous movie stars and established academics; that it may be discovered in the presumptions of authors whose names are known throughout the English-speaking world and, equally, in writers of moronic letters to minor journals. I hope you will agree that the incubus is in the minds of twittish commentators on television and powerful figures in leading national institutions.

In later chapters, I propose to show that this incubus has penetrated the political establishment and has affected official policy. I want to show that there is a dynamic connection between the shared presumptions that compose that incubus and the common disadvantages shared by men which I listed in the Prologue.

But the reader will, by now, be desperate to get answers to the questions which have been bugging every page of this chapter: what is the orign of this universal prejudice? Where and why did it get started, and why has it become so powerful?

THREE

Classes of Evil

People of my generation and of our times adore themselves. We congratulate ourselves upon our accomplishments, our poise and our understanding. We boast about our incomes ('who'd have believed you could get this rich this quick?'), our delicate skills with restaurant menus and with opera house programmes. We know our movies, our records, our books and our way around. We greet each other with the post-HIV hug, loving and enduring, as 'survivors'. We are old veterans from the trenches, out on the other side of the combat lines, grizzled, wearied but still in one piece; and *looking good*.

My question to my contemporaries is this: if we are such delightful people – audacious, clever, educated, literate, loving and hip – how can it be true that we have caused an evil to take shape among us? Are we to be persuaded that we may be as culpably gullible, as vulnerable to totalitarian barbarities as any of those immediate ancestors to whom we thought ourselves so superior by enlightenment and understanding? I reckon so.

The incubus of poisonous intolerance and of totalitarian prejudices which has gathered in the atmosphere between the sexes is our creation. We blew it up, gave it shape and released it. We are responsible for its existence and its effects. The incubus is our own creation. Future generations, I imagine, will be astonished to read their history books in school and see that, in the last quarter of the twentieth century, a generation in the north-west of the planet, in the richest and most advanced countries of the world, took leave of its educated, liberal-minded wits.

Think what we have done.

Consider the intrinsic claims of the feminist propositions to which we have consented: that one half of humanity was inferior, by genetic composition and by natural disposition, to the other half; that the inferior half held the superior half in subjection through the use of economic power and brute force; and that the superior female half was obliged to fight a war of liberation on class lines to emancipate itself from the oppressions inflicted by men and the patriarchal system they enjoyed and supported.

Reading that paragraph, feminists and their apologists and fellow-travellers would say that their beliefs had been grotesquely caricatured. Feminism, they would probably say, has developed so far and has taken so many different but connected forms that it cannot be discussed as if it was a single body of belief and attitude which can be reduced to three cardinal propositions.

I have often heard those responses. They always strike me as being evasive, as dodges and fudges, forestalling argument. If we cannot agree basic terms of definition, we are prevented from arguing further over interpretations: that seems to be part of the purpose of those feminists who refuse to agree that common characteristics, purposes and beliefs can be drawn from all strands and forms of feminism.

There are others, of course, men and women, who say that men have no business at all to discuss feminism and its terms. They say that this subject is, by its nature, exclusively women's concern. They can get off at the next halt. It cannot be admitted, by any stretch of cowardice or complacency, that the exclusive right to set the terms of argument – and, indeed, to conduct the argument – about the social and political relations of men and women belongs to a particular

57

group of women who are attached to a set of shared assumptions.

Despite the evasions of the contemporary sisters, there *must* be a connecting characteristic between all the various forms and styles of feminism, otherwise they would not be grouped together under that umbrella term and the word 'feminism' could have no meaning. In fact, a common denominator for all the forms of modern feminism is quite readily discovered and simply expressed.

Here is my best offer.

The common denominator is the belief that women share interests which are distinct from men's and that those interests can best be advanced by women acting collectively. That much, I submit, must be agreed. No variety of thought or style of attitude could be termed feminist unless it involved these presumptions.

It *is* a tricky business to go further; but I think we can say with confidence that the consequent assumption of all feminism which proceeds from the first point is that women's particular interests are and always have been at odds with the interests of men. Most feminists would go further still and claim that men must act collectively in defence of their own interests to resist the claims and the advances of women.

It amounts to a universal article of feminist belief that women have had to struggle against a political system organised by and for men to achieve freedoms and rights both as a collectivity and as individuals. Many, possibly most, feminists would claim, as triumphs of this struggle, the changes which have occurred in the position of women in the West, especially their emergence as wage and salary earners in the commercial life of the West.

Each of these presumptions, I want to argue, is false. They are false in logic, false in their assessments of social change and its consequences, false in the deductions and conclusions to which they lead.

If you take the point of view I am going to advance, the glories of modern feminism transmute into that filthy incubus. If you look my way into the bottom of the feminist approach, rooting out its origins in the social history of the West and in the writings and reflections of modern feminists, what you will find there is not a set of humane and loving principles discerned with noble intelligence and applied with all the finest distinctions of literacy and judgement, to the advancement of civilisation. What you will discover is a mess of pseudo-Marxist crudities, swirling in a pot of terror, cooking up in an oven of unprecedented social change. You find blind panic disguised as clear-eyed militancy; you find rank selfishness disguised as philanthropy; and you find sophistries of base prejudice disguised as political sophistication.

Step this way.

Everybody agrees that modern feminism, as distinct from the feminisms of the nineteenth and early twentieth centuries, took its origins in the New Left of America and Europe in the second half of the Sixties. There is no argument about that. It's a fact. If you comb the histories of the feminist movement – perhaps the greatest single source of publishing production in this part of the century – you will find arguments and shades of opinion on the precise degree of influence of one leftist groupuscule or faction against another. Was the SDS (Students for a Democratic Society) more influential than the Communist Party? Did the Trots or the hippies first seize upon the ideas? Where stood Rosa Luxembourg or the Witch collective?

If questions like that hold a fascination for you, there is much interest to be found in the library stacks of that history. But the questions need not detain us here. We can agree, since there is no dispute, that modern feminism emerged from that New Left which was largely composed of student radicals.

The question of much greater fascination for me – one which I would love to explore in writing both as an account of those times and of my own life – is: why did so many of the concerns, protests and disenchantments of the young take focus during the Sixties in the political philosophies and terms of expression of the old (Marxist-Leninist) Left?

Why did those CND-ers, Civil Rights marchers, campus malcontents, anti-war protestors and Sorbonne wall-daubers turn in waves and droves to the political analysis of nineteenth-century philosophers and to a world-view whose most powerful advocates were the corrupt old Stalinists in Swiss suits and Italian shoes who occupied the Kremlin?

Here is a question of the deepest personal, political and historical interest; and I would love with all my heart to go into it. But, again, it is not a question which advances the purposes of this chapter and this discussion. We can agree that it happened. The fact that it happened is not in question.

(I cannot resist making an aside on this point: I believe that the radical young of the Sixties turned to Marx and to the Old Left *faute de mieux*. Ignored and despised by the governments and political establishment of the time, by Harold Wilson and his Cabinet as much as by de Gaulle, Lyndon Johnson and Richard Nixon, there was no place for us within the orthodox system of politics. The opposition between the young and the rest was so absolute on issues such as the Bomb, the Vietnam war, civil rights and 'rock culture' – the two sides being mutually uncomprehending and unaccommodating – that we had no place to go but East and no system of belief by which to recognise and organise ourselves other than the certainties offered by the old uncles Karl and Fred. The only other alternative, it is illuminating to remember, was Islam – a path chosen by many black American revolutionaries but one which was not open to the rest of us.)

The biggest problem of political philosophy for those new adherents of Old Left attitudes was to find a class enemy. Revolutionary Marxism doesn't make *any* sense unless the woes and deprivations of groups and classes of individuals can be explained by the operation of the class interests of those who take material and social advantage of them.

Marx himself was thoroughly explicit on this point. Even after 125 years, the clarity of his declarations was to exert a gripping influence on the minds of the young Westerners who were groping for some systematic account of their own alienations and discontents. Marx said:

> For one class to represent the whole of society, another class must concentrate in itself all the evils of society, a particular class must embody and represent a general obstacle and limitation. A particular social sphere must be regarded as the *notorious crime* of the whole society, so that emancipation from this sphere appears as a general emancipation. For one class to be the liberating class par excellence, it is essential that another class should be openly the oppressing class.

and:

> A class must be formed which has *radical chains*, a class in civil society which is not a class of civil society, a class which is the dissolution of all classes, a sphere of society which has a universal character because its sufferings are universal, and which does not claim a *particular redress* because the wrong which is done to it is not a *particular wrong* but *wrong in general*.[1]

---

[1] (N.L.'s italics.) Karl Marx, *Zur Kritik der Hegelschen Rechtsphilosophie Einleitung, 1844*.

By a singular account (mine) the entire history of the Marxist Left in the last 150 years can, narrowly, be interpreted as a quest for the identification of these opposing classes – the class, on the one side, which embodied 'the *notorious crime* of the whole society' and which was 'openly the oppressing class'; and, on the other side, for the class 'which is the dissolution of all classes, a sphere of society which has a universal character because its sufferings are universal'.

Marx's original analysis identified these classes in economic terms and he construed the industrial proletariat as being the 'class which is the dissolution of all classes'. With less clarity, finality and certainty, he identified the 'bourgeoisie' as being the class which embodied the notorious crime.

It is worth looking back briefly on Marx's own difficulties in applying his approach to his own time: those difficulties had become fatal to the analysis as a whole by the time the young radicals of the 1960s tried to apply it.

Marx identified 'three great classes of modern society based on the capitalist mode of production'. They were wage-labourers, capitalists and landowners – the 'three great social groups whose components, the individual members, live from wages, profit and rent respectively, that is from the utilisation of their labour power, capital and landed property'.[2]

Marx acknowledged that, even in Victorian England where these 'great social groups' were readily visible and broadly distinguishable, 'intermediate and transitorial strata obscure the class boundaries'. The working class, dependent upon wage-labour and lacking possession of any other form of capital or of land-ownership, was, indeed,

[2] Ibid.

obvious in its identity. As a class, it truly did comprise the 'mass' of the people, both in the cities and in the countryside. The existence of this class and the economic circumstances and limitations its members shared were commonly agreed and accepted by all sorts of observers, analysts and commentators. It was not necessary to be a Marxist to subscribe to that common view.

Beyond that consensus, however, lay perplexing complications of analysis and identification, chiefly in the difficulties of pinning down the economic powers and position of members of the 'bourgeoisie' who might, simultaneously, appear to be members of more than one class. A doctor might have nothing to sell but his labour power; but his circumstances could not readily be matched with those of a factory worker, especially if that worker owned property or had inherited capital.

Members of landowning families might be personally impoverished, might be dependent upon their wage-labour as government officials. Were they to be described as members of the 'bourgeoisie' if they lived in rented property and accumulated no capital to bequeath to their children? How could the peasant farmer or kulak be described as a capitalist or a landowner when the sum of his possessions and 'stored-up labour' amounted to a donkey and a hectare of land?

These 'intermediate and transitional strata' did present taxing difficulties for Marxists who were looking for an enemy class to oppose and to vanquish.

Marx had said that the general emancipation of society depended upon 'a certain class' which 'is felt and recognised as the general representative of society. Its aims and interests must genuinely be the aims and interests of society itself, of which it becomes in fact the social head and heart.'[3]

---

[3] Ibid.

The 'certain class' was the industrial proletariat, whose existence everybody could agree. The problem for Marx and his followers who sought practical applications of his theories was to identify and extirpate the enemy class, the embodiment of the 'notorious crime'.

That effort was more easily done with conviction than said or written with persuasive plausibility. It gave specious reason to many of the most loathsome and diabolical episodes of savagery in this century. Stalin's massacre of the kulaks and his forced deportations of millions of his opponents to labour camps and to death were accounted for and rationalised on the grounds that those individuals were members of the enemy class. The same totalitarian logic was given to Mao Tse-Tung to explain and to justify the hounding and murder of professional and semi-professional people in the Cultural Revolution. The same barbaric lines of reasoning were given by the Khmer Rouge when they force-marched the inhabitants of Cambodian cities into their killing fields.

Philosophical distinctions presented no obstacle: the tyrants bludgeoned through the 'intermediate and transitional strata' which Marx had acknowledged, hacking and shooting a path of expedience through those complications in truth which blurred distinctions of class and might frustrate the application of Marx's theory.

By the late Sixties, in the West those complications in truth had become thoroughly disorientating for all would-be followers of Marx. The difficulty now was not simply to identify the enemy class. Still more taxing was the task of naming the class of heroes whose 'aims and interests must genuinely be the aims and interests of society itself, of which it becomes in fact the social head and heart'.

The industrial proletariat, so readily identifiable in the nineteenth century, had extensively decomposed by the

64

middle of the twentieth century. High-paid workers who had stored-up capital in freehold property, insurance policies, pension funds and shareholdings could not convincingly be portrayed as members of a class whose deprivations have 'a universal character because its sufferings are universal'. Who, in any case, was the proletarian? A dentist's receptionist could be said to have her hands on the means of production only in the most remote and negligible senses. Her financial standing would put her closer to the factory worker than the dentist; but should she be described as a member of the factory worker's class rather than the dentist's – in whose class she would probably prefer to see herself? Beyond these complications lay the bewildering changes in the technology of industrial production which had, themselves, obscured divisions of class between workers and managers. In car factories, for instance, it was already happening in the Sixties that foremen and even line-managers were expected to share some of the tasks and all of the working conditions of their subordinates.

Meanwhile, traditional heavy industries which employed legions of proletarians were entering a visible decline in output and numbers of employees; and, simultaneously, the industries of media production, financial services and sales were calling for ever greater numbers of highly qualified workers whose salaries and other forms of remuneration were making them into a new class of capitalists.

How to make sense of it all? How could the old axioms of the whiskery uncles be applied to this baffling variety of change and still emerge as the eternal verities and fixed horizons of political landscape for which the young were yearning?

In the early years of the Sixties, when masses of the young began to edge leftwards, the old axioms and shibboleths were aired anew with, frequently, comical or grotesque results. I remember that when I first came across members of the Young Communist League in 1963, when I became a sixteen-year-old local official of CND, they tried to tell me, in all solemnity, that the Berlin Wall had been erected to keep out the hordes of starving Westerners who wanted to break into the East. I remember, too, the venomous disapprobation of those comrades when I started stepping out with the glamorous daughter of a local publican: I had, to their way of thinking, made a fatally compromising connection with the bourgeois enemy.

The confusions and ideological strangulations of those hopelessly muddled youngsters in Salisbury, Wiltshire, came out of grander difficulties of abstract thought which were also occupying the minds of bigger thinkers across the West. Herbert Marcuse was one of the first political philosophers of the time to recognise that modern Marxism must respond to an imperative need and adjust its class perspectives. Marcuse, Ernest Mandel and others argued that, following the distintegration of an industrial proletariat and the blurring of other classical lines of distinction, a new class had to be identified which should be the 'class which is the dissolution of all classes'. New skins were needed for the old whine.

Marcuse and Mandel saw the promise of this new class in the immense body of students in institutions of higher learning all across the West. In the second half of the Sixties, many of the more florid and unconvincing effusions of campus radicals took their diction and their style of reasoning from Marcuse's vision. The idea that the London School of Economics and other centres of learning might become 'Red Foci', in the style of Maoist and Cuban guerrillas, proceeded, so far as I can remember, from Marcuse's apothegms. It may have been a potty notion but, at least, it was grand in vision and grandiloquent in expression. The least noble effort to apply this style of thought came, to my mind, when Cambridge undergraduates declared that it was a revolutionary act to complain about the quality of the food they were served in their dining-halls.

While the Marxist bottle of theories with its Marcusian cork was bobbing around more or less harmlessly on the seas of student radicalism, it was also lifted as a Molotov cocktail in a far more dramatic theatre of the political world.

Around 1966–7, led by Stokely Carmichael and Eldridge Cleaver, the idea first got put about that a class division existed between blacks and whites in America, giving rise, in theory, to a revolutionary prospectus in the headquarters of capitalism and at the centre of the liberal world.

Here, for sure, was a potent and compelling application of the old paint. 'The *notorious crime* of the whole society' of the United States was, in lurid and incontestable shades, the second-class citizenship of coloured peoples. The segregations of blacks, the denial of their political rights, the scale of their poverty and the extent of their deprivations made a perfect picture for political enlargement. For a brief moment in 1967–8, it was easy to see the blacks as the Black Panthers wished to describe them: 'a sphere of society which has a universal character because its sufferings are universal'.

The snag, as ever in this approach, was to find and define the villain. Which class of individuals in the United States could be named as being 'openly the oppressing class'? Who was to blame? Who was the enemy?

The enemy, came the answer, is *within* ourselves, not merely a limb of the body politic but an essential component of our very own being. The enemy is 'white culture' and whites are, by birth, agents of that culture. It followed that the enemy, honky reader, is yourself. Thus spake Eldridge Cleaver and Huey Newton, LeRoi Jones and, to some degree, James Baldwin.

The Black Power movement of the later Sixties was the first overtly Marxist movement of the modern West to express the claim that an ineradicable evil could inhere to groups of individuals who had nothing in common but their birth. Seizing the bludgeons and cleavers of totalitarianism, they carved their way through the problem of 'transitional strata' in the enemy class by saying that it didn't matter what *you* thought, said or did: if you were born white you were, irredeemably and unalterably, a member of the oppressor class. You were, by your birth and existence, guilty of the notorious crime and, it followed in the mind of Eldridge Cleaver and some others, any black might revenge himself for that general ill by assaulting you individually.

It was – need it be said? – a monstrous and wicked perversion, an insidious, corrupting and pernicious falsification and falsehood.

Nonetheless and to the eternal shame and disgrace of the nincompoop generation of love and peace, the falsification was enthusiastically accepted: the perversion was given place; it took hold and, with consequences which have done much to spoil our lives and to inhibit our powers, it held.

It is a puzzle now, twenty-five years later, to account for the impact of that Black Power casuistry, to explain the instantaneous collapse of liberal principle and desire among the white Westerners who endorsed that totalitarian hokum. Why was it found to be so compelling among young liberals who had devoted their energies and their passions to the elimination of disadvantages for blacks and of the brutal and hateful prejudice with which they were surrounded? Why were those educated young whites so willing to declare themselves guilty? Why were they so eager to see themselves as the enemy?

These are, again, questions which contain the most absorbing interest to my mind; but they are, I regret, off the chart of this book and its purposes. If you know the history of that period, you must agree that the Black Power propositions were advanced and were embraced. If that history has passed you by and if you want to check it out, you will find hundreds of books and documents which give its records. You might like, for instance, to look at the writings of Carl Oglesby, Angela Davis and Dotson Rader. You can go as far as you like. Be warned: it's gloomy and heavy work.

As briefly as I can, I want to offer the suggestion that young whites were eager to see themselves as the enemy because the proposition drew and set the limits on an accessible and comprehensible political universe. Part of the appeal of the Black Power sophistry lay in its implicit claim, soon to be extracted and paraded on placards, that the political realities of the outer world could be discerned in the inner life of the individual and in his or her personal relationships with others.

That outer world was infinitely unmanageable, implacably impervious to protest and to reason. The universally shared feelings and desires of the young were, visibly, held in contempt. It simply did not make any difference to, for instance, the conduct of the war in Vietnam how many hundreds of thousands of the young demonstrated their opposition in the capital cities of the West. Argument over the manufacture and deployment of nuclear weapons made not a jot of difference to the insane policies which decreed their manufacture and deployment. In the shining city on the hill of Western democracy, Presidents and presidential candidates were being regularly rubbed out in the most suspicious circumstances, suggesting conspiracy conducted at the highest levels of government, and those murders were being hosed away from public attention from a faucet of official bullshit and lies.

In these aspects of political life and in all others, the young had no power at all to influence the counsels of the elders. They were ignored. It is enormously revealing to see, for instance, that the condensed edition of Richard Crossman's diaries of the deliberations of Harold Wilson's Cabinets 1964–70 records, throughout that period of massive disaffections among the young, only one brief discussion of unrest in British universities. That discussion took place in March 1970 and the Cabinet agreed that Vice-Chancellors should be stiffened by government support in their duty to root out troublemakers.

In retrospect, it is astounding that Labour politicians who prided themselves, above all, on their management of dissent in the party should have been so blind to the consequences for their own party of a mass defection of their own natural supporters among the educated young. But that's how it was, both in Britain and elsewhere. We know that Lyndon Johnson was thoroughly mystified by the militancy and the passions of the young Americans (mostly natural Democrats) who bellowed their opposition to the war in Vietnam over the garden rails of the White House. We know that he and de Gaulle were able to comprehend those passions and the demonstrations they ignited only as evidence that a Red plot was being spread throughout the West. Otherwise, the young made simply no sense to their leaders.

The cardinal tenets of Black Power made the outer world comprehensible, if not manageable, within personal and domestic life. When the Panthers said that their objective was 'bringing the war back home', they offered young whites a prospectus of political action within a theatre where their powers were visible and from which they could not be excluded: the family and its psychological life.

The slogan 'the personal is political' is broadly assumed, these days, to have been invented by modern feminists, by whom it has certainly been appropriated (see Rosalind Miles above). It was not so. The slogan was drawn from Black Power apothegms which described the origins and the intrinsic powers of racialism within the psychological and family lives of white Americans.

The Panthers set off a spark of unreason which instantaneously caught fire across boundaries of sense and across cultures. It was on the lips of Berlin students at the barricades and it was current among the Paris Situationists of 1968 and elsewhere some moments before 'the notorious crime' committed against women as a whole was identified. The first time I heard a young radical express the idea that it would be a revolutionary act to kill your parents was in October 1968, in Cambridge.

The speaker was a boy, the son of a powerful senior executive in the advertising company J. Walter Thompson. He and a group of his friends were pleased to call themselves The Bash Street Kids. Under the influence of a lot of LSD and other psychotropic drugs, their political interests and concerns had reduced to the aching vibrations within a straining cranium. Since the 'personal was political' it followed that 'it's all inside your head, man'.

Madness lay that way: we tripped gaily out along the path, declaring en route that madness itself was the only sane response to an insane world.

Gripping as they were, the analytical propositions of Black Power were limited by the special conditions and circumstances of blacks. Those conditions could not be represented convincingly, however hard the imagination of the radical young tried to see them as such, as 'a sphere of society which has a universal character because its sufferings are universal'. The sufferings of the blacks were – at length it had to be admitted – particular to themselves rather than universal to the whole of 'bourgeois society'. Blacks *were* excluded, segregated, refused admission to the institutions of state and to all but the most menial and slavish work. We – the young whites – were not.

It was fun to see ourselves through the clouds of ganja and the thump of soul sharing the universal conditions of the blacks; but it had to be recognised (not least because they told us so) that their particular deprivations and ills were their own special inheritance. Given this limitation and prohibition, the bogus diktats of old uncle Karl were discarded on the wayside of American society so far as the plight of the coloured peoples was concerned. Anyhow, the radical young had discovered a much more exciting use and focus for those rusty old blunderbusses.

They were immediately picked up, dusted off and re-directed, with infinitely greater power and conviction, as the philosophical and analytical tools and weapons of the Women's Liberation movement.

In *Sexual Politics*, first published in 1969, Kate Millett declared that recent events (which she did not name) had, at last, compelled a recognition that relations between the races in America were, indeed, political relations which involved the general control of one broad group, united by birth, by another broad group, also united by birth. Such groups, given power by birthright, were disappearing quickly, she said; but there remained a distinct and ancient 'scheme' for the control of one group by another. A disinterested examination, she said, would show that the same state of relations existed between the sexes as between the races – a relationship of domination and subordination which Max Weber described as *Herrschaft*. Males ruled females, she claimed, by a birthright priority and they had, thereby, achieved a most ingenious form of 'interior colonisation'. This form of colonisation was, she declared, stronger than any other type of social segregation and more vigorous than other forms of class distinction. The dominion of females by males is, she said, our culture's most pervasive ideology, providing it with its most essential ideas and conceptions of political power.

Millett's declarations can be taken – as indeed they were employed – as the loci classici of modern feminism. They confirm what I have been trying to argue and to show: that the presumptions of the New Left as to the circumstances of blacks jumped the rails and were applied, as articles of canon law, to the circumstances of women.

The long wander of the Marxist Left through the institutions and societies of the modern West, in search of the class which would be the head and heart of society, the class which would be the dissolution of all classes, had culminated in the definition of 'the birthright priority whereby males rule females'. The lost tribe had found its Israel and its new Moses. The totalitarian classifications of the old nineteenth-century big beards had, with a vengeance, come back to roost at home. Karl, meet Kate: Kate, this is Karl: you two were meant for each other.

Kate Millett's diction is unmistakably that of a Marxian of the old school. To speak of 'a disinterested examination of our system of sexual relationship' is to employ the rhetorical devices of doctrinaire Marxists in all generations (Who says the examination is 'disinterested'? How do we know that there is 'a system of sexual relationship'? On whose say-so are we to take these terms for granted?)

Her sentiments contain an almost eerily accurate reflection of Marx's original prescription. He had called for the formation of a class which could be a 'sphere of society which has a universal character because its sufferings are universal, and which does not claim a *particular redress* because the wrong which is done to it is not a *particular wrong* but *wrong in general*'. Millett provides the answer to this call with her ingenious form of 'interior colonisation', which she describes as being more rigorous than class stratification and as supplying our prevalent cultural ideology and most fundamental notion of power.

The essential articles of Kate Millett's opinions swept the Western world. Nothing in our time matches the speed and breadth of the intellectual movement she initiated. Never in our lifetime has a prescriptive analysis, penned and advanced by a diligent academic caught such fire in the minds of a general public across international and continental frontiers. Within a score of months after publication of *Sexual Politics*, Millett's point of view and her specific terms had entered the lingua franca of a host of writers in America and Europe and had been accepted, as commonplaces of conversation and observation, by the vast horde of malcontented young radicals across the West.

Heaps of examples can be given of this spread of universal assumptions. My table, at this moment, is supporting thirteen texts from that period which overflow on every page with the presumption that Kate Millett and the women she inspired had identified a classical and eternal verity and a dynamic point of departure for a revolutionary prospectus. Let me put my hands on a few of them, just to sketch that scene.

In her 1969 essay 'On American Feminism', Shulamith Firestone described the aim of the new feminism as being the overthrow of the oldest, most unbending caste/class system in existence which is based on sex, consolidated over thousands of years, and lending the archetypal male and female roles an undeserved legitimacy and apparent permanence. She spoke of the new feminism as being the beginning of a long struggle to break from the oppressive power structures set up by nature and reinforced by man.

In 1969, Margaret Benston contributed to *Monthly*

Review an article called 'The Political Economy of Women's Liberation'. She wrote:

> The 'woman question' is generally ignored in analyses of the class structure of society. This is so because, on the one hand, classes are generally defined by their relation to the means of production and, on the other hand, women are not supposed to have any unique relation to the means of production . . . In arguing that the roots of the secondary status of women are in fact economic, it can be shown that women as a group do indeed have a definite relation to the means of production and that this is different from that of men . . . If this special relation of women to production is accepted, the analysis of the situation of women fits naturally into a class analysis of society.

To complete this set of darts, let's turn to that trusty old quiver, that repository of all that is most contemptibly ego-serving, malignant, posturing and false in the canons of modern feminists, the thoughts and words of Dr Greer. In her Summary, which was the prelude to *The Female Eunuch* (first published in 1970), Germaine Greer predicted that:

> the most telling criticisms [of her work] will come from my sisters of the left, the Maoists, the Trots, the IS [International Socialists], the SDS, because of my fantasy that it might be possible to leap the steps of revolution and arrive somehow at liberty and communism without strategy or revolutionary discipline.
>
> But if women are the true proletariat, the truly oppressed majority, the revolution can only be drawn nearer by their withdrawal of support for the capitalist system.

Ah, Dr Greer: the Lord love you; where should we have been without you? Yours is the Gibraltar of cant by which we can steer through the straits of this argument.

If it is true that 'women are the true proletariat, the truly oppressed majority' then all the nightmare excesses, the poisonous hostilities and vicious aggressions of the last twenty years may be excused, even if they cannot fully be justified. Self-evidently the victims of oppression, especially if they are in the majority, cannot be expected to act kindly towards their oppressors, to show tolerance, restraint and good will. If their distinct and justifiable interests are thwarted by a class of oppressors who employ totalitarian means to continue and sustain their power, who can object if the oppressed ones revolt violently in the advancement of their interests? The sympathies of all right-thinking people must, incontestably and by the rules of natural justice, lie with the oppressed.

But what if – let the question germinate – what if it is *not* true that women are the proletariat? What are we to make of those violent effusions, those hectoring marching songs and rallying cries, if – give way to the doubt – it may not be true that women are the truly oppressed majority? Never were; never have been; never could be. Then what?

Let's inch our way towards those questions. This is a perilous course of navigation, heavily mined with fiendish and submerged devices. The clearest way through to an open Atlantic of argument is to keep your right eye on that rock of doctoral cant and your left eye on the sure contours of that list of disadvantages which I assembled in the Prologue. Remember, always, that we have seen that institutionalised disadvantages for men are widespread in the formal patterns of domestic and family life in Britain. We have agreed – have we not? – that a society which includes such disadvantages cannot be named a patriarchy.

76

Now let's train our sights on the enemy at hand, while steering for the distant but clear horizon.

In the paragraphs of *Sexual Politics* which follow immediately after her identification of the *Herrschaft* between men and women, Kate Millett gave the particular context of explanation for that general relationship. An order of sexual dominion is sustained, she said, because our civilisation, is like all civilisations throughout history in being a patriarchy. We could not mistake this recognition, she said, if we looked at the institutions of power in our society – the armed forces, police, industry, technology, universities, science, political office and finance – and saw that they were all in the hands of men. The essence of politics being the control of power, she said, 'such realisations cannot fail to carry impact.'

We may agree that the essence of politics is power. Sure. We may not disagree for an instant that, at the time when Millett was writing and still, largely, today, every institution of power is in male hands. No contest. The point of argument and division arrives in the last words of the paragraph. What is and should be the impact of those realisations? Do they truly mean what they mean in Millett's mind – that our society, like all other historical civilisations, is a patriarchy?

Millet tells us that patriarchal government is an institution which affords control of the female half of the population to the male half. The institution (is it that?) operates, she says, on two principles: the first is that the male shall dominate the female; the second is that older males shall dominate younger males.

These points add up to the depiction of a system of control and of oppression which is purposeful, willed, deliberate, chosen and intentionally inflicted by males upon females. According to Millett and to all of the disciples who have followed her down the decades, the direction of every avenue of power was and – to the extent that it remains – is in male

77

hands because that's the way men wish, choose, require and compel our societies to take their shape and exercise their powers.

'Patriarchy' thus became 'the notorious crime' prescribed by Marx. Throughout all the writings of the early New Left feminists, emancipation from the sphere of patriarchy, to borrow Marx's terms again, was represented as a means to bring about a general emancipation. Germaine Greer was always characteristically emphatic and concise on this general perspective and the specific terms of antagonism it involved. 'If women liberate themselves,' she wrote, 'they will perforce liberate their oppressors.' In a number of places throughout her writings in the early Seventies, she openly declared war. 'Men are the enemy', she said in *The Female Eunuch*. 'Men are the enemy', she wrote again in an essay published in February 1970. 'They know it – at least they know that there is a sex war on, an unusually cold one.'

The justification for this belligerence was held, per se, to be the existence of patriarchy. A syllogism of the most brutal (and, one may say, anti-Marxist, anti-historical) illogic was the casus belli that gave shape to the rules of engagement. If all power was in the hands of males it must follow that males had chosen to exert those powers over women: therefore it followed, further, that women were obliged to wage war against men and their system of power in order to obtain for themselves their due and just share of powers both political and economic. The war of liberation to obtain those powers would, necessarily, involve the defeat of the oppressive system and a general emancipation.

The presumption that men chose to operate a system of powers that excluded and took advantage of women is the common coin of modern feminism. It is, in fact, the sine qua non of the intellectual movement which has been, beyond compare, the most influential and demanding force in our times. The presumption can be seen to run beneath the entire literary landscape of modern feminism. It stretches from Eva Figes and her book *Patriarchal Attitudes* (published in 1970) to Naomi Wolfe and her book *The Beauty Myth* (published in 1990). It leads from the measured, pseudo-scientific terms of Juliet Mitchell in her late-Sixties writings in the *New Left Review* to the spit-flecked ravings of the gauleiter Julie Burchill in her journalistic columns today. It is the common denominator of the psychotic denunciations of Valerie Solanas in *The SCUM Manifesto* (published 1968) and of the self-contented vanities of Kate Saunders in her book *Revenge* (published 1990).

Throughout all those writings – and, I suggest, in all the casual and conversational terms by which men are universally described – runs the presumption that a political system of 'patriarchy' is conducted as an elective conspiracy of men for the purposes of sustaining their own powers.

What, the reader must ask, is wrong with the idea?

Self-evidently, women have never, until the present day, been admitted as equals – either in numbers or in powers – in the institutions of modern societies. Even today, it is obvious that women who seek advancement in those institutions face considerable difficulties (I shall want to consider them). It is beyond argument or dispute to say that all post-nomadic societies have confined women in one form or another of domestic ghetto – usually without material rewards or rights. Nobody can deny – why should they want to? – that in all Western societies down to the present age, political and economic powers, honours and distinctions, titles, perks and pride of ownership have been the sole property of men.

What, then, is the argument? Where is the dispute? If all those points can be so readily conceded, it must appear that the feminist case wins by a walkover. We agree that men have had power and that women have had none. If that division of powers does not describe a patriarchy, what on earth is it?

It is not a patriarchy.

The presumptions of Kate Millett and her cohort run along a fault of logic and a rift of sense as wide, deep and potentially destructive as the San Andreas fault. A tremor of scepticism will touch it off and then the citadels of dogma erected by the feminist orthodoxy all along the way may slide into a Pacific of impassive history.

Let me apply the first gentle touch by asking what might have made the post-war generation of women so special that they were able to discern and to vanquish a universal system of oppression to which hundreds of millions of their fore-bears, in all ages and generations, had submitted? What made them so clever and their sisters through all eternity so dumb?

This is not an original question. It has occupied the minds of many feminist writers and they have produced screeds of answers. One of their answers is to say that women had never, before the post-war era, been educated in great numbers in universities and other institutes of higher learning. Women, goes this answer, had been denied the intellectual apparatus and the tools of analysis by which they might comprehend the wider workings and the true nature of their particular and individual oppressions.

This answer seems to imply that you've got to have a degree in sociology to realise when you're being screwed.

Another answer, sometimes given by the same people who advance the first explanation, is that women, in all ages, *have* resisted the oppressions of patriarchy but the history of that resistance has been, until lately, kept a secret. The women's movement, in its efforts to establish and to vindi-cate that history of struggle, has created an entire industry of scholarship, both in publishing and in academia. All the

Centres of Women's Studies have, in part, taken their raison d'être from the claim that women had a particular history of their own which women themselves should be entitled to explore and to expand on their own terms. I want to attack that claim in detail in later pages but, for the moment, let me say that even if it were true that women's particular consciousness and their special history of rebellion had been suppressed by patriarchal powers, it is still rather peculiar that women in all ages down to the nineteenth century should have done so little to protest about or, in organised movements, to resist those oppressive powers. I mean, 5000 years is quite a long stretch of suffering under the 'notorious crime' without it being universally acknowledged and resisted, wouldn't you say?

What, I ask again, was so special about Western women in the Sixties? What was the difference between them and all their ancestors in all times? Forgive the previous teasings: let me ask this question in all seriousness.

Was there, in the lives of women before 1965, any simple reason – natural, given, intrinsic to their lives and independent of the operations of political institutions – why they could not participate in public life on equal terms with men? Kindly ask yourself further: what changes occurred in the lives of women in the West in the years 1965–70 to remove any obstacle which had previously prevented or inhibited their emergence into public and commercial life on equal terms with men?

Answers:

1. The Pill.
2. Abortion by dilation and vacuum curettage.

The reason why men had all the powers and women had none in all Western societies until the late nineteenth century was that women could not, with any degree of certainty other than by total abstention, control their

81

fertility. The reason why women were enabled, in the mid-Sixties, to emerge from the confinements of their domestic ghetto was that, at precisely that date and for the first time in all of human history, women were provided with a technology which gave them infallible control over their fertility.

What the feminists chose to call 'patriarchy' was, in all its expressions (including romantic love and men's systems of clubs and honours), nothing more than a set of social relations and conventions which arose from, expressed and refined a division between men and women which was, until the Sixties, essential, natural and ineradicable.

Yes, it did happen that a culture emerged from that division in which the powers of men were celebrated, in which they were widely believed to be superior, in which women and children were defined by law and custom as the property of men. Yes, indeed.

But the reason was not, essentially and primarily, that men invented that culture to suit themselves and to keep women down. The reason was that if women were to have babies, if the tribe was to reproduce, a system of concessions was required which allowed for the cardinal uncertainties of women to know when they might become pregnant and for how many years they might be suckling infants. Marriage, itself, was instituted as one such concession (see the marriage ceremony in the Book of Common Prayer).

I will argue, throughout the remainder of this book, that all the social institutions and conventions which had defined the relative positions and roles of men and women had been determined by that cardinal uncertainty. Unless they were unmarried or wholly chaste within marriage, individual women *could not* be admitted to social life outside the family on equal terms with men. Societies, I will say, had been so extensively organised to accommodate those concessions and the particular needs of pregnant and suckling women that the opportunities they afforded women for activity in the society beyond the family – even for those women who were chaste – were, necessarily, limited and few in number.

Until the introduction of abortion techniques by the safe, quick and barely fallible method of dilation and vacuum curettage, pregnant women had never been able to determine, without risk to their lives, whether or not they would carry a baby to term. This incapacity, again, ruled women out for admission to forms of social life outside the family on equal terms with men. I will argue that the introduction of this technology and of the technology of contraception were essential to the labour requirements of modern market economies and that they were falsely perceived as a vital weapon of liberation in the 'sex war' women are required to wage against patriarchy.

The introduction of these inventions and technological innovations marked a division in human affairs which was without precedent. The few years, less than half a decade, in which they became freely available to a broad public throughout the West were a watershed in history more dynamic and divisive than the invention of the spinning-jenny or the introduction of the steam engine. Those brief years were a moment of history more directly influential in the lives of all individuals than the moment when the geniuses of Los Alamos exploded the first atomic bomb. Nothing which went before, in the determining circumstances of women and in the general state of relations between men and women, need, necessarily, be true for those future circumstances and relations after the introduction of infallible contraception and safe and quick abortion.

The introduction of the Pill and of safe abortion has, it goes without saying, occupied a great deal of attention from feminists and has been the subject of much argument and

83

disagreement. Even so, it is very striking that the historical importance of these inventions has not been considered among the central propositions of feminism. No feminist author, as far as I know, has taken the view that it was the contraceptive revolution rather than the consciousness of women, charged with militancy, which changed *everything*. On the contrary, those inventions have been seen as side-issues.

Parts of Betty Friedan's book *The Feminine Mystique* were first published in magazines in 1963 and the book emerged as a whole in the immediately following years. By that time, the existence of the Pill was well-known, even though it was not yet seen as an invention which would rapidly transform all personal and social relations between men and women and would confound, disrupt or overturn all the expectations, traditions and conventions by which they had been accustomed to see themselves and each other.

The word 'contraception' does not appear in the index of *The Feminine Mystique*. 'Planned Parenthood' gets one entry, in the first pages of the first chapter (where the author muses over the sudden increase in births in America in the Fifties). 'Birth Control', similarly, appears once only; and that in the Epilogue, which was not written and published until 1973.

Betty Friedan takes it as axiomatic that women have 'a right' to demand effective contraception and easy abortion. She speaks, as many of her successors were to speak, as if the facilities of contraception and abortion might be withheld from women as ways of keeping them in their place and might only be prised from the ungiving society by women wielding the crowbars of their feminist consciousness. In other words, Friedan implies that the impetus towards change for women came from the desires of women, rising as a collectivity, rather than – as I see it – those desires and, indeed, that rising being initiated and facilitated by the technology, without which they could not exist. Friedan says:

> Society had to be restructured so that women, who happen to be the people who give birth, could make a human, responsible choice whether or not – and when – to have children and not be barred thereby from participating in society in their own right.

This passage thrums with presumptions which I shall want to question further (such as: Why should anybody think that having a job equals 'participating in society in their own right'?); but I am interested, for the moment, solely in Friedan's view that 'society had to be restructured', through the provision of contraceptive and abortion technology, to afford women that right.

This is the established view of the feminist orthodoxy, that women had to battle to get the benefits of the contraceptive revolution as an intrinsic, but not fundamental, element of their general war of liberation. It was, in their book, a small pocket of conflict on the long front line of emancipation. As Sheila Rowbotham put it, in her history of British feminism entitled *The Past is Before Us* (published 1989), 'In the course of the struggle for the freedom to separate sexuality from giving birth, the abortion campaign involved challenging laws and the structures and practices of medicine, technology and science.' Of all feminist authors and commentators, only Shulamith Firestone and Juliet Mitchell (so far as I know) took the view that the contraceptive revolution, in and of itself, fundamentally altered the position of women. Sheila Rowbotham herself quoted from Juliet Mitchell's 1966 article 'Women: The Longest Revolution', where Mitchell had said:

> Once childbearing becomes totally voluntary, its significance is fundamentally altered . . . The fact of overwhelming importance is that easily available contraception threatens to dissociate sexual from reproductive experience – which all contemporary bourgeois ideology tries to make inseparable, as the raison d'être of the family.

Sheila Rowbotham wrote a line of commentary upon these views which I take to be the prevailing feminist opinion. She said, 'In practice, the development of contraceptive technology was to be less transformative than Juliet Mitchell envisaged.'

Well, I suppose it depends what you call transformative. Whatever that word may mean, I think it must apply to the development of that contraceptive technology as it arrived in the Sixties.

What would we have thought if we had been told in the Fifties that, while we were still young, an invention would be introduced which allowed any woman to have sex with any man she chose without risk of pregnancy? What would we have thought if we had realised that this invention led automatically to the possibility that women could go to work on equal terms with men and that men could take equal responsibility and power in the home? How would we have viewed the future if it had struck us that this invention made redundant all the laws and taboos, the conventions and the courtliness by which all societies had tried to ensure that the father of a woman's child should recognise the child as his own? All the wooing, the yearning and the romance; all the paraphernalia of infatuation, the promises, the pinning and the ringing? All the particular confinements of women, the ring-fences of convention which secured them in sexless suburbia, their hobbling shoes, their hair-dos and their nail-paintings – all blown away? All the guilt and shame and public approbrium which went with a premature loss of virginity or an enthusiastic taste for adultery – all irrelevant, pointless, unnecessary, gone?

We would certainly, I think, have called it a vision of transformation. At least.

Would we have been pleased to know that ours would be the generation which would see and implement that transformation? Or might we have been daunted just a touch, wishing that this could happen to somebody else instead, that we might just hold up these changes for a while, deny their 'transformative' powers at least until the hormonal riotings of our own youth had quietened down a little?

It fell, of course, to women to bear this weight of change: not all women; just a very big group. Women who were over the age of forty in 1965 were largely exempted from the changes which were just about to break upon the world. Women born after 1970 would enter a world which had already adjusted very broadly to the convulsive changes which had occurred. But there was a particular class of women, born around the time of the Second World War, who were caught dead in the middle of the sea change. To those women, it fell as an acute task and responsibility to negotiate a set of demands for personal and social change such as no women in the entire history of human beings had ever had to face.

No wonder a lot of them funked it. No wonder they tried to erect an ideological Berlin Wall which would restrain and deny change. No wonder they created a hysterical dogma which was intended to keep men in their place and women in theirs, even while it was advanced as a prospectus for revolutionary change by which individuals might be released from the imprisonment of sexual stereotypes.

The people who advanced this contradictory ideology had

87

already shown themselves capable of believing anything. Among them, in fact and truth, were those young nitwits from Salisbury who, a decade before, had told me that the Berlin Wall was erected to keep out the hordes of Westerners who were clamouring to get into the socialist dream state. Now, erecting their own wall and parading their banners upon it, they were going to say that reaction was change, that the tyranny of sexual stereotyping (the one they chose) was emancipation and that hate was love.

You could call it *Sisterspeak*.

FOUR

Blind Panic

'We were all young, nearly all in our twenties. None of us had a job. None of us had a husband. Hardly any of us had a child. We hadn't had to deal with any of the real complications of adult life.' *Rosie Boycott, one of the founders of the feminist newspaper* Spare Rib, *in conversation with the author in August 1991.*

Here are a few facts. They need to be chewed slowly and digested fully before we move on to the richer repast of argument. They are drawn from the records of British ministries and official statistics for England and Wales. The pattern they describe was duplicated throughout north-western Europe and North America.

Between 1965–1975, the number of women received into institutions of higher learning in Great Britain rose from 4884 to 22,784. Between 1961–1977, the number of married women in Great Britain's labour force rose by 77%, bringing an extra two million workers into employment. The number of abortions rose from 22,256 in 1968, the first year in which abortion was made legal, to 139,702 in 1975. The number of divorces granted rose from 27,000 in 1961 to 80,000 in 1971.

In the following decade, many of these figures altered less dramatically. The decisive change had occurred. The number of women in the workforce actually fell slightly, by one or two per cent, between the mid-Seventies and the early Eighties. The total number of women in higher education in

1970 was 178,200: in 1980, the number was 202,800. The number of legal abortions rose from 139,702 in 1975 to 171,873 in 1985. Compared with the trebling of their numbers in the Sixties, divorces merely doubled between 1971–1981, from 80,000 to 157,000.

Feminists of all sorts presume that the changes which occurred in the position of women in the second half of this century resulted from the claims of the women's movement and the militancy with which those claims were advanced. Very many of them (see the *Guardian* Woman's Page any week, hear 'Woman's Hour' any day) really do think that there are more women doctors, lawyers, teachers, broadcasters, businesswomen and truck drivers today because the Sixties' sisterhood demanded that it should be so. The figures I have recorded tell another story.

It was *institutional* change which transformed the position of women – new laws, regulations and practices which passed, with flabbergasting speed, through the political establishment of the day. The quintupling in the numbers of women received into universities resulted from the Robbins Report of 1963. Abortions rose sevenfold in number in a single decade following the Abortion Act of 1967, which itself resulted from David Steel's Private Member's Bill for which a sympathetic government provided parliamentary time.

Figures for divorce trebled as a direct result of the 1969 Divorce Reform Act rather than as a consequence of altered states of consciousness.

The introduction of those reforming laws and practices had nothing at all to do with the women's liberation movement. Just nothing; that's all. No connection. The Acts, in most cases, were passed *before* the voices of Kate Millett, Ti-Grace Atkinson and Germaine Greer began to be heard. Those parliamentary acts grew out of the political consideration of social needs – considerations which themselves long preceded the acts of the legislators. For example, the need to broaden admissions to British universities, to build new universities to meet the needs for an expanded managerial class in the post-war economy, had been generally recognised and agreed from the mid-Fifties. If it had not been so, the reforms recommended by the Robbins Report could not have been implemented, as they were, before the Sixties were out.

In retrospect, two features are most striking about these changes. The first point of amazement is that they were introduced and passed into law against negligible opposition. The transformations which occurred in official attitudes towards women's education, their place in divorce and their right to have an abortion were all introduced into the mainstream of the official life of Britain without crisis.

It is customary to see these changes as resulting from vigorous campaigning by interest groups against the entrenched opposition of a backwoods establishment. It doesn't look that way if you read the records now, nearly thirty years later. What appears much more noteworthy is the scale of agreement and consensus in British society on the need for these changes. If a patriarchal order of establishment had existed, would it not have acted more forcefully to defend and to conserve its interests? Compare the Corn Laws repeals and reforms.

The second dazzling point of interest is in the overwhelming magnitude of those changes. In retrospect, it is clear that an unprecedented and largely unrecognised revolution occurred in the central nervous system and all the cells of our lives.

In the late Sixties and early Seventies, our society took the full impact of a fissiparous shock for which it was entirely unprepared and to which it failed, pitifully, to adjust with patience, understanding, tolerance and restraint. The shock was administered, with shattering abruptness, directly upon the War babies and the post-War generation. They, both men and women, were largely left to their own devices to come to terms with the fall-out from changes which none of our ancestors had ever encountered.

The direct predecessors, our own parents, could not draw from their own experience to comprehend the scale and the impact of the changes which had arrived. Having, in their own youth, fought a world war which caused the deaths of twenty million people and which included, in its final stages, a vision of the end of all life on earth, they were entitled to feel that the lives of their children were a cake-walk by comparison with their own. Those children had been born and had passed their infancy in a world of domestic stability, high employment and material luxury. What could they (we) possibly have to complain about?

The parents would say, with towering complacency, that the teenagers of the Sixties and the young adults of the Seventies acted as if they had invented sex. In point of fact, there *was* some truth in this line. A new world of sexual relations had been invented, not by the young themselves but by the chemists and technicians in the laboratories of California where the contraceptive pill was refined. That device exploded over the West with fissive and devastating effect. At the epicentre of its explosion stood the young men and women of the post-war generation. They would be marked for life by its blast and its fall-out. It blew them apart.

The contraceptive pill having been invented for women, it naturally appeared that they were, exclusively, the recipients and bearers of change. All their expectations and conventions having been exploded by the device which took its place in their handbags and on their bathroom shelves, it was understandable that the focus of public attention should be directed upon their condition, as they demanded that it should be. Men, it was assumed, were essentially the same as they had ever been. Men, I believe, assumed this too.

I assumed it myself, of myself, until the last few years. The gulf of understanding between my father and me was, I reckoned, easily explained and measured in terms which were universal to men of our different times. He and I might, as we did towards the end of his life, quietly lament the distance between us but it was the result of historic movements of social change which were beyond us.

Clothes and hair, music and drugs, political allegiances and money came into the picture between us, aggravating our differences and inflaming rows. Between my cocky vanities and his middle-aged impatience, these knick-knacks and cosmetic differences were taken to be major issues of ideological division; and the silence which fell between us from my late teens to my late twenties, from 1965–1975, was seen by both of us, I believe, as being preferable to our incessant, raging disagreements over correct attire and voting intentions.

Everybody knows this story: there is nothing new or unique to me in it – which is why I am telling it. The same story, reflecting the same dimensions of division, might be told by a hundred million men across the West. I must have exchanged parts of this story in conversation with a thousand men of my own generation. When we were younger, we congratulated each other and ourselves on the division from our fathers which we reckoned we had brought about as a kind of revolutionary act. The last thing on earth we wanted was to be like our fathers. We were so smart. They were so dumb. In later years, as the fathers have inched towards their graves and as the sons themselves have become fathers, some measures of self-mockery and of contrition have been detectable among the accounts of the men of my generation. Was it possible that such a very big deal could have been made out of the width of a flared trouser-leg or the height of a Cuban heel? Isn't it a bit sad that the very education which lifted us out of our fathers' class should have made it impossible for us to talk to each other?

Only in the later years of the Eighties, by which time my own father had been nearly silenced by ill health, did I begin to realise that the seminal point of division between us had not been class, not books, not money and occupation but sex. In our sexual lives, we had been forced to inhabit separate worlds. I had grown up in his world and I did know something about it. He knew nothing of my world and could not enter it. Even if we had been able to overcome our inhibitions and our modesties, even if we had been able to discuss our personal and sexual lives, he could not have comprehended mine.

The scale of division between us can be rendered by a simple head-count (or perhaps it is not heads which are being counted here). My father married my mother when she was nineteen and he was just twenty-two. It is more than likely that each was the other's first lover; but even if that was not the case, it seems very unlikely that there might have been more than two or three others. Before he died, my father assured my mother that he had never had intercourse with another woman throughout the fifty years of their married life. Whether or not this was true (I believe it), I think it is extremely improbable that my father might have had sex with as many as ten different women in the whole of his adult life. In all probability, my father's sexual life would have replicated his own father's experiences.

I had complete intercourse with a girl for the first time when I was just eighteen in October 1964. Five years later, in October 1969 when I met the woman who was to become my first wife, the count was ten. By 1975, when I met my second wife, I had lost accurate count. The total, I knew, ran

94

into more than three dozens but any list I compiled contained quizzical uncertainties ('Did she and I actually *do* it? What was the first name of that fat girl? Or the last name of that thin girl?'). The women I was in bed with would sometimes tell me that they had the same kind of trouble.

I do not think I was unusual: I believe mine were the usual experiences of my generation. Some boys might have gone further than mutual masturbation with their girlfriends and lost their virginity at an earlier age; some might have had more lovers than I in their early twenties. Those few who married when they were very young did not, presumably, enjoy or endure the promiscuous opportunities which came my way in my mid-twenties. Taken as a whole, however, I would guess that my story roughly matches the individual stories of tens of millions of those Western men who are my direct contemporaries in the post-war generation. I know for sure that my story largely accords with some hundreds of other men with whom I have talked it over at some time or another.

Ours had become, truly, another world. None of our fathers had ever known the variety of sexual opportunity which was ours for the having – no mistresses, no kept women, no prostitutes, no servant girls. No resulting babies. Our lovers were our equals and our contemporaries. They were women whom we might, in earlier ages, have wooed, affianced, married and monogamised for life. They became, instead, our dancing partners for a single fuck, for a few dates or for some months of cohabitation. There was – need it be said? – chastening misery as well as delight in this wealth of sexual opportunity and many tears were shed, not only by the girls.

Our fathers thought a few tears were a trifling penalty. Ours was a world which they had glimpsed in fantasy. They saw us, I think, as the Frank Harrises they would have been if their imaginations and their purses had matched the capacities of his. If our fathers knew anything of our sexual lives, their least equivocal responses were those which ached with bitter envy. We had entered the years of our adolescence confined by sexual and marital expectations which had been common to men in all generations for a century, since the introduction of the condom. We had emerged from those years bearing caskets of sexual riches which had previously been reserved for princes and sultans.

Like our ancestors, we began our teenage years at the beginning of the Sixties with identical prospects. We could look forward to an occasional touch of brassière hook, stocking top or suspender in our mid-teens. We would lose our virginity, swathed in a condom and a sweat of terror, towards the end of our teens. If an accidental insemination had not propelled us to the altar before we were old enough to vote, we would make a monogamous marriage in our early twenties, for the sake of regular sex and legitimate babies. We would work for forty-five or fifty years to support our wives, with whom we could expect that all sexual intercourse would cease around the time the kids left home and she arrived at that time of life.

We looked forward to adulthood with resigned desperation, knowing that we should, infallibly, reproduce the grim, toiling and sexless lives of our fathers, that the way to the straitness of that prison gate was fixed and undeviating. No wonder that we counted ourselves as blessed, presented with the keys to pig-heaven, when – in the mid-course of that progress, right on the dot of our twenties – the girls got the Pill and the way was cleared to every nipple and beyond every stocking top (within a matter of moments, by the summer of 1967, they had discarded stockings and bras altogether).

It was some kind of heaven, at that moment, to be a young

man and to know that this unprecedented and all-involving change must necessarily alter all the traditions and functions of manhood. If we didn't have to have babies when we had regular sex, it followed that we didn't have to get married. And if we didn't have to support families, we didn't have to have jobs or careers; and if we didn't have to have careers . . . what might we not do? Or be? A tabula rasa of adult masculinity had been presented to us, upon which we might (we supposed) make our marks as we pleased.

At some moments, between 1966–69, it appeared that the most perfectly divine opportunity had been given to us. We did not *have* to be our fathers. Judging by the signs of those early times, our style of masculinity would be markedly less aggressive, martial, competitive and self-denying than the soldierly styles of our fathers.

Pacifism was, already, a widely endorsed and oft-demonstrated principle among us. How many boys of the Aldermaston age and after, those Idi Amins in duffle-coats and baggy pullovers, dreamt of parading in the passing-out ceremony at Sandhurst? Or the Police Academy? We had already, before the mid-Sixties arrived, voiced a common disquiet over orthodox career prospects. Who wanted to be the Man in the Grey Flannel Suit? We had already embraced the ideal of sympathetic partnership with women, rather than endure the brutal antagonisms and miserable bitchings which marked our parents' married lives. Yearnings for change were deeply felt among young men before the instruments of change were delivered, only to be appropriated by the peremptorily demanding class of young women for the purpose of keeping us like our fathers.

Among the first and most noticeable changes which occurred after the widespread distribution of the Pill was that men suddenly looked a lot more like women. The hair and the beads and the floral shirts, the floppy hats, the furs and the shoulder bags and the high heels were all worn with pleasure by heterosexual men as well as by homosexual men (both men and women would say that it had become much harder to know, on sight, where a man's sexual tastes might lead him and you). Delicacy, both of body and of feeling, was prized. Skinny T-shirts, narrow-hipped jeans and pointy-toed boots looked best on a small-boned body like Marc Bolan's; they looked riciculous, like a turtle stuffed into a snail's shell, on a shot-putter's back or a slob's big beer gut. It was, similarly, hip among boys to express confusion rather than to dictate certainty, to be the hung-up and incoherent victim of conflicting emotion: not to know what to think, what to want or who to fuck.

The outlines of conventional masculinity altered immediately when the contraceptive pill was introduced. That coincidence goes beyond chance, in my mind. I take it now, as I took it then, that the invention of the Pill invited us to compose ourselves, individually, according to our own conception of masculinity. To that degree of possibility and of freedom, the moment *was* heaven.

It didn't last two seconds. The incubus was cooking up in its pressure-pot of terror and was about to blow the lid. Very many of the sisters were very far from happy. They did not welcome or approve of uncertainty. They required moral rules and firm categories of gender definition. They had ideas of their own as to the nature of masculinity and the eternal, changeless needs and functions of men. They were, moreover, going to make absolutely sure that their ideas should hit home and be felt there.

Even before the totalitarian simplicities of Marxian class dogma began to emerge from feminists, voices of modern women had been heard expressing a generalised disgust about men and deep uncertainty about the lives and the place of women. Nell Dunn's book *Talking to Women*, published in 1965, is an invaluable source of record for those voices, which spoke for a set of fashionable attitudes. She recorded interviews with nine women, aged between their mid-twenties and mid-thirties, living in London, mostly married. Throughout these interviews, if you read them now, you can find the strains of the times, as they were felt by women.

In conversation with Edna O'Brien, Nell asked if Edna knew the difference between right and wrong. Nell explained that she asked the question because, she felt, one of the problems of their generation was that 'everything seems to have gone from under our feet'. The women agreed that they felt insecure because 'we have no moral code' and 'didn't know what we are meant to be doing'.

A perfect moment, bespeaking an entangled mass of the perplexing confusions of those times for women, came in the conversation between Nell Dunn and Emma Charlton who was twenty-nine and the mother of two young children at the time of the interview. Nell asked Emma if she thought that women are any different from men. Emma answered that she thought they were entirely different. 'I don't understand men at all,' she said. 'I don't really like men actually.'

Nell agreed and she said that she cared far more about the good opinion of women than that of men. Emma concurred that she didn't really care what men thought about her. Even so, she said, she still found herself trying to gain a man's approval and saying things to please him, even if she was not attracted to him. 'But that's really a form of looking down on them because I wouldn't do this with a woman. It's really just appeasing them, to keep them in their place or something.'

A woman who did not like men would go out of her way to

be attractive to a man, 'to keep him in his place' even if she did not find him attractive. A woman who cared much more what women thought of her would stop talking to a woman if a man came by. Given the choice, she said, she would prefer to interest herself in the woman: she did not feel, evidently, that she had that choice.

Within five years of the publication of *Talking to Women*, the disquiets and disturbances which Nell Dunn had recorded were assembled and codified in a Marxian catalogue of revolutionary prospectus. While the prospectus as it was launched by Kate Millett and seized by Germaine Greer was, ostensibly, based upon a platform of universal truth and ideological certainty, it took a good part of its impetus from the much less grand and rather more particular and temporal difficulties of individual women of that age in finding and establishing their place, in knowing the place of men or understanding their desires. The complaints which those early ideologues uttered were mirrored in the headline questions of teeny magazines: 'What does he want? Will you let him have it?' Or 'Virginity: The Prize Nobody Values' (I am making these up; but they probably appeared).

Shulamith Firestone, who was saluted as one of the more accomplished, lucid and learned feminist revolutionaries of that time, expressed this conjunction of personal confusion and ideological groping, in a paragraph of her 1969 essay 'On American Feminism':

> In the Sixties the boys split. They went to college and Down South. They travelled to Europe in droves. Some joined the Peace Corps; others went underground. But wherever they went they brought their camp followers. Liberated men needed groovy chicks who could swing with their new life style: women tried. They needed sex: women complied. But that's

all they needed from women. If the chick got it into her head to demand some old-fashioned return commitment, she was 'uptight', 'screwed-up', or worse yet, a 'real bringdown'. A chick ought to learn to be independent enough not to become a drag on her old man [trans. 'clinging']. Women couldn't register fast enough: ceramics, weaving, leather talents, painting classes, lit. and psych. classes, group therapy, anything to get off his back. They sat in front of their various easels in tears.

'Some old-fashioned return commitment'? Tears in front of the easels? Could it have amounted to this? Holy smokes alive, I thought we were supposed to be dealing with the emancipation of the commonalty, here. I thought we were identifying the class which should be the dissolution of all classes. Is this serious; or what?

The girls were very serious. They really did feel that a case could be made for the revolutionary overthrow of all bourgeois society out of the upset felt by post-adolescent girls over the inattentiveness and disobliging behaviour of their favourite beau ('He just wants me for one thing only, otherwise I'm not a human being to him. I'm *so* upset'). You think that's a florid exaggeration, a mean-minded and typically callous (male) barbarity. Take a look at the record.

The single complaint most frequently aired by women's liberationists in the early days was that, in radical groups and organisations, they were expected to be docile and servile and lick stamps. If you trawl back through the books and papers of that time you will find the great stamp-licking question at every major juncture of the early rise of the movement. The manifesto of the women's caucus of the National Convention of SDS in 1967 declared, in its second point: 'We call upon the women to demand full participation in all aspects of the movement from licking stamps to demanding leadership positions.'

This phobia about stationery and gum found its place in the deliberations of young radicals all across the Western world. The stamp question – who franks? who licks? – was vented in Paris in 1968 and in London in 1969 with as much passion as the question as to whether the car-workers of Ford or Renault might join the students on their barricades. I'm *not* making this up. I was there, on that scene. It was my patch. Take my word for it.

I remember also that the demand was conceded, with negligible resistance, wherever it was raised – even if it did not truly reflect the realities of the women's roles and the regard in which men held them. Some macho fantasies in the berets of Che Guevara and the leather bombers of the Black Panthers muttered about the duty of the chicks to serve their men; but anybody who tries to make out that the young men of the time were insistent that the young women should be restricted to secretarial duties and secondary roles needs to take another and straighter walk through the archives and through their memories. Young men of that time did not wish the women to be like their mothers any more than they wished, themselves, to be like their fathers. They did not believe that they had inherited, nor did they desire, dictatorial powers. In the radical movement of the young, as elsewhere throughout the society of the day, the need for mental adjustment to the changed position of women was so broadly recognised that there was, effectively, no argument. No contest. Men sought change in and for women as much as they sought it for themselves. We were all, don't forget, optimists.

The sisters were determined not to take 'yes' for an answer. They insisted on seeing resistance where there was none. An implacable and deathless enemy stalked their psyche and they were dead-set on manifesting that enemy in the outer world. We need to remember something which we appear to have forgotten or overlooked: they were all very young women, facing enormous difficulties which were, uniquely, their own.

Not until I began to write this chapter had it ever struck me that nearly all of the major figures of the women's liberation movement, the leaders in print and in meetings and demonstrations, were just out of their teens when they cast their doctrine upon the world. Most of the seminal writers, such as Germaine Greer, Sheila Rowbotham, Shulamith Firestone and Kate Millett, had barely grown out of their post-doctoral breeches. None of them was an established writer with a body of work behind her. In nearly every case, the book with which they made their name in the rapidly expanding bibliography of modern feminism was their first work. In America, Gloria Steinem had made her name known to a limited group of readers and editors through some magazine journalism. In Britain, Beatrix Campbell was known – in a decidedly limited circle – as a sub-editor who occasionally contributed articles to the *Morning Star* (formerly the *Daily Worker*). Apart from those women, the writers who advanced a manifesto for revolution against the most insidious and deeply entrenched system of human oppression in the whole history of the planet, nay the cosmos, were without achievement of any significance or professional reputation of any standing in the world.

Is it possible that a group of 25-year-olds might be given such attention if they emerged today or at any other time in this century?

Give this question some air. Let it expand. Imagine that a group of thinkers and writers took shape today, all in their mid-twenties, claiming to have latched on to a perspective of analysis which explained an eternal and previously misapprehended structure of institutional society, one which accounted for the misdemeanours of Cromwell and the stylistic infelicities of Hemingway as much as for the man in bed at home who did not care enough for your clitoris and its essential requirements. What would you say?

We know what you would say; so we have to ask ourselves a few more questions. Why *were* those young women taken so seriously? What were their particular and pressing claims for public attention which made their general propositions, so fantastic and so juvenile in retrospect, plausible and persuasive at the time to a general society?

They *were* a group so extensive that they amounted not to a class but to a sub-class, powerfully united both by specific interests and by collective emotion. That is what I want to say and to argue. That is the best explanation I can give and the only way I can see to make sense of it.

They *were* not all women, though they claimed to *speak* for all women. They were, in fact, a very definite and very large group of women whose individual circumstances were shared by others of the same age throughout the West. Their particular difficulties, rather than being the same as those faced by all women in all times, were unique to their own times and their own generation; but the mutant version of classical Marxism to which their authors adhered required them to say that they were joined, in sororal interests and plights, with all women in the present and, through their historic sufferings, with all women in the past.

They were the Class of Sixties women: an authentic sisterhood.

They were the ones who had been born around the time of the Second World War. They were, or they became, broadly speaking, middle-class. They had received the benefits of the educational reforms of the Forties and Fifties which took them into sixth forms and universities. They were, simul-

104

taneously, the victims and the privileged recipients of the institutional changes in the position of women which had accompanied or resulted from the contraceptive revolution. *Poor Cow*, the title of one of Nell Dunn's plays, was a good name for them.

They had grown up with common and conventional expectations of adult life which little differed from the lives of their mothers and grandmothers, including monogamous married love, maternity and housekeeping. They had been taught to cherish their chastity and give the prize of their maidenhead only to the man they would marry. They had learned, in childhood, the vital women's business of pleasing a husband, from making a Sunday lunch to looking decorous at a cocktail party. They might have been laying away treasures in their bottom drawer throughout their adolescence. They had been taught to expect that boys should do all the paying and all the driving and that, if you didn't keep your hand on your halfpenny and make sure that they kept their hands on the wheel and their eyes on the road ahead, all the hell of a teenage pregnancy would be the instantaneous outcome.

These same girls found themselves, in the later Sixties, facing the overthrow of all those expectations. They found themselves expected to take a job *and* to have an opinion on a better hob, to desire a career, to experiment with multiple sexual relationships, to defer childbirth. Most of all, they found themselves the vessels of a technology which afforded them absolute and infallible protection against pregnancy; and, if they slipped up, they could take advantage of a safe and speedy technique for abortion.

It now appears to me that those changes, demands and expectations threw that generation of women into a blind panic. 'Everything', as Nell Dunn said in 1965, seemed to have gone from under their feet. They had, as Edna O'Brien

105

observed, no moral code, no fixed and absolute points of certainty by which to recognise themselves, from which to take a fix on their future lives and their social position.

In the absence of moral certainties, the girls composed their own code. It blended the ageless diction of the unhappy woman ('They're all the same, those men! Bastards') with the revolutionary huffing and guffing of the New Left. Seeing their painful perplexities as the outward symptoms of a universal system and themselves as the class to end class, they sought the enemy and his class to blame. The one who was nearest to hand was the Eric Clapton lookalike in the corner of the room, with his beads and his bells, his copy of the Kama Sutra in one hand and his erection in the other hand. That sucker was asking for it. Who the hell did he think he was anyway (God's gift to women), calling for a dish of pulses and steamed courgettes while he applied his acid-soaked brains to the taxing man's business of figuring out the strategic reserves of General Giap? This boy needed to get a few things *straight*.

It is wonderfully comical now to look back on the earliest claims of the sisterhood as they began to raise their voices in the early Seventies. That such a God Almighty big deal could have been made out of sock-washing, spud-peeling and the cleansing of lavatory bowls! That scrubbing floors, choosing sausages and dusting cornices should be connected, as forms of oppressive labour and deprivations of the soul, with the plight of Vietnamese women working in rice-fields under a sky filled with B-52s or with the miseries of slave women in Detroit ghettos! Senses of proportion and of humour went missing all along the sisterly front-lines, both in the fox-holes of the launderette and the command-posts of the kitchen.

I know that this picture taxes credulity, that it looks like a spiteful caricature. If you don't know or can't remember

106

exactly what happened in those years, I do urge you to look it up. A good guide is Sheila Rowbotham's *The Past is Before Us – Feminism in Action since the 1960s*. She recorded that 'It was amazing how extensive were the questions which came from such an apparently humdrum matter as housework. You start off with a mop and bucket in the kitchen and end up reorganising the world in ways that most gentlemen philosophers had not deigned to imagine.' Amazing.

In her first chapter, which sites the origin of the women's movement in Britain in domestic dissatisfaction, she quotes from a woman's poem about a man's mother:

> I've met your mother and know just what you want of me.
> Dinner in the oven and washing on the line.

For this woman and for many others quoted in Rowbotham's first chapter, the horror of being condemned to repeat the lives of older women and mothers was the impulse which drew together the sisterhood and caused them to discuss forms of union and ways of life which might burst the bounds of domestic confinement. Intrinsic to this picture was the idea that men demanded domestic service of their women and would brook no alternative.

Remember who these women were: they were not their mothers and their men were not their fathers. Those men, those boys, contemporaries of the sisters, had lived alone in flats or student bed-sitters; they were, in hundreds of thousands and in millions, to continue to live as bachelors for longer stretches of their adult lives than their fathers. They were capable of running their own domestic lives; they could cook, often as well as the girls; they managed their own laundry; they did not suppose that it was a woman's automatic and exclusive duty to scrub the kitchen floor or clean the lavatory bowl. These boys *never* thought that it demeaned their manhood to push a supermarket trolley or a vacuum cleaner. It was and is preposterous and silly to pretend otherwise.

Not *one* of my contemporaries at university in the late Sixties or the young men I met when I went to work in London entered the Seventies in sexual or spousal union with a woman who was a domestic drudge. I'm talking about maybe 500 chaps of that age: you might even call them 'typical males' of their age and class, the same age and class as the sisters. In the last twenty years, none of those men has, to my knowledge, sought to make a match in which a woman was required to enslave herself in domesticity. Even if they had wanted such a union – which desire none of them ever expressed even when bonding with each other in intoxicants – they couldn't have afforded it. The women with whom those men have coupled have been required to work, often against their expressed desires, to provide for the expenses of the joint household. A few of those women have refused to do their full share of paid work, to the bitter distress of their men who would gladly have exchanged a better class of cuisine for a pay-cheque regularly deposited in the joint account.

The sisters in Sheila Rowbotham's book were flapping their dusters at a shibboleth and a chimera. The man they were assailing was an old bogyman, not present among us even as we were on the cusp of that incandescent change of life between the pre- and post-Pill societies of the West.

According to my own memories, it was they – the girls – who found it harder to adjust to the new divisions of domestic life which had been thrust upon us. In the mid-Seventies, very often women visiting me in my flat would ask the name of my very good cleaning-woman; when I had no cleaning-woman. 'Who gave you the flowers?' they would demand, when nobody had given me the flowers. My cooking was never more than slightly less primitive than a caveman's; but my standards of household cleanliness were a sight more fastidious than a good number of those women's (as were, in some cases, I may add, my standards of personal hygiene).

This probably sounds like swanking. Can't help it: it's true. A more general picture is given in two sentences from another woman quoted in Sheila Rowbotham's first chapter who said: 'My husband has accepted a fairer division of the housework fairly happily. More difficult has been my own attempts to stop acting out the role of a wife.'

If the sisterhood was going to advance a critique which described all women as being oppressed by all men and their patriarchal system, they had to turn to women other than themselves and to circumstances other than their own. Through this curious double-helix of necessity, the personal was rendered as being political not in the personal lives of the individuals who espoused the theory but through their imagined accounts of other lives, other classes, other times. They turned, first, to a received, classical – and historically outmoded – account of the family and of the father.

Enter Uncle Fred.

Engels was a firm favourite among Marxian feminists at the turn of the decade. He was the St Paul, you might say, of the orthodoxy which proceeded from the writ of *Grundrisse*. His vision of the family was lifted, in large parts, straight into the pages of Kate Millett's book *Sexual Politics* – from which it became a standard tool of dissemination across the West in the next ten years.

Kate Millett's account of Engels in *Sexual Politics* pro- vided, again, the locus classicus of feminism's point of view. She had defined women as being 'a dependency class who live on surplus' and, thus, a class subordinated within the system of patriarchy. She went on to say that the family is the chief institution of patriarchy, 'a patriarchal unit within a patriarchal whole.' She spoke of the traditional powers by which patriarchy gave fathers rights of ownership over women and children, even allowing them the right to beat them, to sell them or murder them. Kinship is property, she said, and in the system of patriarchy the father is the owner.

When Millett was writing in the late Sixties, none of this had been strictly and completely true of Western societies for a century. Married Women's Property acts, Marriage Acts and a sheaf of divorce law reforms had, even before the Second World War, extensively mitigated the property rights of fathers in families. Incontestable rights of physical abuse or the murder or sale of wives and children had been eliminated by statute in all Western societies over centuries. The 'classical' system she identified had incontestably prevailed all across Europe for most of 1000 years; but by 1969, when the book was published, the few surviving remnants of that 'system' were already on the way out. If the feminists had not been so adamant in insisting that they denoted a permanent aspect of social relations, those remnants and the attitudes they connoted might – by common consent and willing agreement – have been swept entirely into statutory redundancy in the coming decades. They were, however, essential to the feminist propositions. They secured and conserved the place and the interests of men.

With an almost daughterly deference, Kate Millet gave Friedrich Engels unmitigated respect and unlimited authority for having provided a complete account of patriarchal history and economy. She praised that account as being the most radical ever published, saying that Engels had been unique among theorists in denouncing the system of patriarchal family organisation.

She honoured him for seeing that the oppression of women could not be described simply in economic or political terms but amounted to a broader 'total' phenomenon, a way of life

110

which required to be expressed in terms of what she called 'class emotion'. She quoted Engels at length:

> The first class antagonism appearing in history coincides with the development of the antagonism of man and women in monogamy, and the first class oppression with that of the female by the male sex. Monogamy was a great historical process. But by the side of slavery and private property it marks at the same time that epoch which, reaching down to our own days, takes with all progress also a step backwards, relatively speaking, and develops the welfare and advancement of one by the woe and submission of the other.

The feminist writers such as Germaine Greer who followed Kate Millett copied her in quoting a key passage of Engels. But they usually gave an abbreviated version of his full observation, which Millet quoted in its entirety. In *The Origin of the Family, Private Property and the State*, Engels wrote:

> The modern monogamous family is founded on the open or disguised slavery of women, and modern society is composed of molecules in the form of monogamous families. In the great majority of cases the man has to earn a living and to support his family, at least among the possessing classes. He thereby obtains a superior position that has no need of any legal special privilege. In the family, he is the bourgeois, the woman represents the proletariat.

When Germaine Greer lifted these words of Engels to reproduce them in a block in *The Female Eunuch*, some peculiar modifications and excisions appeared. The passage was rendered as follows: 'The modern individual family is

111

founded on the open or concealed slavery of the wife . . . Within the family he is the bourgeois and his wife represents the proletariat.'

No doubt the change from 'woman' to 'wife' is simply explained by the differing translations and editions from which Millett and Greer were working. But Dr Greer's exclusion of the intervening sentences is the work of a deliberate hand. Why, the reader should ask, did she excise those words?

They were, it would seem, distinctly inconvenient. Engels, writing in 1844, was describing an economic condition and a state of relations within marriage which were passing, with electric speed, into historical redundancy by the time Greer chose to make use of them. The great majority of cases were changing so radically that it was already clear that women as well as men would have to work to earn a living. In the joint-income couple which would be the only option for men and women who chose to live together, both individuals would be the bourgeoisie. Who, then, would be the proletarian?

Germaine Greer dodged this question by apparently skipping it. A truly remarkable number of her followers who quoted Engels chose the same solution to the same problem: they cut the heart out of it. Why should they worry? Who was going to notice or object to an authorial sleight of hand in those days when any man who expressed a doubt about the truths of feminism was automatically and screamingly denounced as 'pig', 'misogynist' and 'male chauvinist'; and any woman who declared herself unconvinced was reckoned to be a candidate for 'consciousness raising' (as if she couldn't possibly know what she was talking about, poor bitch)? Part of the purpose of that hysteria was to make sure that the terms which the feminists advanced should be incontestable, pure and certain.

What they needed, to stop the earth moving under their feet, was an agreed and fixed point of understanding for themselves and for their men. They chose to unearth that fixed point from the earth which was erupting most convulsively: the family. As with so many aspects of the feminist approach, theirs was a perverted post hoc account and rationalisation of changes which had already occurred or were occurring at the time.

We have seen that the figures for decrees absolute given in divorce courts in Britain trebled in a single decade between 1961 and 1971, making marital breakdown a common event in national life where it had previously been rare. Most of these divorces were granted to men and women in their twenties and thirties. The parents of those individuals had treated divorce as a disgrace and a horror, an extreme and distressful solution to impossible conditions. For those people, acts of adultery were threatening to the substance of the marriage contract, since those acts might result in the births of illegitimate children. Adultery was, therefore, an offence against marriage which required an automatic response from the courts. The survival of the tribe and the health of the nation demanded that the guilty partner should be named and ostracised; the guiltless one must be exonerated.

The introduction of infallible contraception vitiated the offence of adultery at its root. If sexual intercourse outside marriage need not involve the risk of children being born, the act of adultery need not be seen, automatically, as offering a threat to the essential substance of the marriage contract. The Divorce Reform Act of 1969 left adultery on the statute books as an automatic cause of dissolution; but it removed much of the stigma which went with adultery and it was correctly described by its opponents as an 'adulterers' charter'.

The institution of marriage was transformed, with consequences which were inevitably transforming for family life. Couples were not to be bound to each other, indissolubly and exclusively, for five decades of monogamy. Children born within one marriage were not – for better or worse – to be bound exclusively to the two adults who had solemnised that marriage but might find themselves, throughout infancy and adolescence and even into their own adulthood, accommodating a number of different figures who had some degree of parental standing. They might be living under the same roof as a number of other children of the same mother but of different fathers, of the same father but different mothers. In every aspect, the traditional nuclear family with two adults and 2.74 children was – even as the feminist assault on that traditional orthodoxy was being mounted – disintegrating.

While the overall character and the constituent elements of the family were changing right in front of our eyes, the women's movement took a style of address to the 'institution' which made it out to be a fixed monolith like the Maginot Line. They took it to be an institution of patriarchy, preserved to benefit capitalism even while the institution was taking thoroughly new forms, perhaps in response to the requirements of modern capitalism. They sought the means to subvert this institution, 'to break through to new relationships', as they kept saying, even while those thoroughly new relationships were being forged in the chaos of change which was indifferent to their claims. In *The Past is Before Us* Sheila Rowbotham records this exercise:

> During the 1970s, however, the impact of capitalist society on women's position in the family was discussed in the women's movement most extensively in terms of work, relations and value. The family as a

114

place of work, and the division of labour which placed the onus of housework on women as a sex, gave rise to a great body of feminist theory. The theorizing in turn raised a whole series of questions. How did it come about? Had it always been so? How had other societies solved the problem of producing goods, bearing children and caring for dependants? These enquiries took off into the 'large domains' of history and anthropology. Feminist searchers did not always return with clear answers – but the generation of such questions revealed how extensively male-defined priorities had ordered intellectual definitions.

Those graduates and post-doctoral scholars bent their minds to making a connection between themselves and others who did not, could not, share their particular circumstances and difficulties. In the routine style of all lefties in all generations since Marx, they turned first to the working class, both in the present and in the past.

Extending the claims of sisterhood, they tried to make out that the excruciating poverty and gruelling conditions of toil of working women, such as the seamstresses in north of England garment factories, illuminated an aspect of the oppressions of all women. In the lives of those working women with husbands who were, emphatically, not pram or supermarket trolley pushers, those men who did expect to have a hot meal served to them promptly on returning from work and who felt that the changing of a nappy was the work of women and pansies, the sisterhood claimed to see the abiding demands and requirements of all men in all ages. Every time a working-class woman said that she was her wits' end with her fella and, for two pins, she'd brain the bugger, the sisterhood elevated her as a heroine of the movement and danced around her complaints as if they were an ancestral totem.

The sisterhood did not, in fact, make much more than a slighting impression on the poor or on the working-class women with whom they sought to join hands. Their failure to make any deep and lasting difference in the circumstances and the ways of life of poor women, especially poor young women, is one of the most marked and damning of all the failures of feminism and I shall want to go much further into it in a later chapter. Suffice it to say, for the present, that in the population at large beyond the privileged middle classes, women are still expected to be responsible for most of the household tasks of cleaning, cooking, shopping, laundry and child care; while men are still almost exclusively responsible for the house, car and garden maintenance and repair.

In that very large sector of the population where cohabiting men and women are both employed full-time, there has been a dramatic movement in the graphs of demographers towards a sharing of the routine, daily tasks of domestic maintenance, both cleaning and feeding. At the same time, even in that sector, duties of childcare are taken mostly by women and the manual work of maintenance on property remains almost entirely in male hands.

In the wider society, therefore, it would appear that changes in the division of domestic labour have taken place, when they have occurred, in response to the economic exigencies of the family as they have been imposed by the workings of the labour market. Where families have been removed or insulated from those exigencies, the pattern of their activities has remained stubbornly the same as it was.

As far as I know, the graphs and figures do not exist which might show what happened in the homes of the young middle classes from which the sisterhood emerged. I can only depend upon my own observation and the stories I hear. Those observations suggest that, in the homes of double-income professionals, where the demands of career have been felt as keenly for the woman as for the man, a great weight of domestic duty has been shifted into the hands of servants and auxiliaries.

In those couples, women have continued to do more of the cooking than their men and, perhaps, more of the washing and ironing. Other duties, especially those of household cleaning and childcare, have been shrugged off into the laps of a great army of 'dailies' and nannies, au pairs, neighbours and grannies.

Engels had said that, in the modern (i.e. nineteenth-century) family, the man was the bourgeois and the woman the proletariat. If we wanted to revise that remark today, we would have to say that the modern middle-class family is founded not on the slavery of the wife but on the slavery of a mass of poorly paid, unskilled, mostly ununionised, mostly propertyless supporters and servants. Most of these indi-viduals, including baby-minders and play-group leaders, are women and they constitute a lumpen class, within an underclass. But the exploitation they suffer is not the exploitation of women as a class.

They are exploited not by reason of their gender but because of their economic subservience. Within today's modern family, the parents (earning mothers and fathers) are the bourgeoisie and the nanny is the proletariat. In those millions of households where a single woman is caring for children, the state is father. Within this system of arrange-ments, nobody is likely to be happy – not the men, not the women, not the children, not the slaves, not the state.

The idea that middle-class women should employ domestic servants for household responsibilities fell into some desuetude between 1940–1970. Mrs Miniver might have her faithful daily and the children might go to boarding schools but it was broadly assumed that individual adults ought to be able to conduct their domestic lives without the labour superventions of servants. If the middle classes retained cooks or domestic cleaners, they felt (see *Look Who's Coming to Dinner*) some unease that they were enforcing, for their comfort, some degrees of impoverishment and degradation upon poor people who might be better employed in open commerce. No doubt this fashionable unease was partly explained by shifts in the labour market during, between and after the wars. That was the era when demand for labour moved, in half-decades, from slump to boom and from the full-employment of all hands in wartime to the more leisurely and prosperous days of the Fifties when all available jobs were occupied by men and women were employed in the work at home which had previously been performed by menials.

But the social trend away from the employment of servants also had some connection with broader notions of egalitarianism and of personal self-sufficiency. The higher good of the general society and of the poor in particular was enhanced, it was agreed, if all families shared roughly the same needs and duties and fulfilled those responsibilities themselves. The domestic drudgery of the middle-class woman in the suburb was not viewed as a confining force of self-denial in America or in Britain in the Fifties: her labours, matching her less prosperous neighbour's, were, by universal consent, seen as being a step towards a new Jersualem of classless equality, endued with much the same kind of optimism which surrounded the building of big municipal housing estates. A Festival of Britain spirit hung in the pelmet boards and it was shined by the dusters of the woman of the house. The classes were drawing together. The brow-beating bewilderments of the middle-class couple over the right choice of Electrolux refrigerator or Suffolk Punch lawn-mower were duplicated in the deliberations of working people over a Sunbeam kettle or a Pye radio. We all had

118

lunch at the same time on Sunday. We all ate the same ingredients. Father came in from the garden. Mother cooked.

However benighted and impoverished a picture of personal delight and social emancipation the suburban vision may have been (few might argue), it did eliminate to a degree the requirements of the middle-class home for servants. Those requirements resurfaced in spades in the late Sixties and Seventies, when middle-class women went to work in millions. A new underclass of domestic menials came into being to support the holy rights of an individual to serve corporate institutions and of markets to make money. In some parts of the sisterhood, the creation of this underclass was seen, most oddly, as a necessary function of female emancipation.

In 1990, I attended a small conference of women doctors which had been organised to discuss the particular difficulties of women in the health service. One of the speakers was the radical gynaecologist Dr Wendy Savage. She gave a speech outlining the history of women pioneers in medicine who had entered the profession over the last century. When she described the prolific energies and deeds of Elizabeth Garrett Anderson, she went out of her way to stress the numbers of servants retained in Elizabeth Garrett Anderson's home. Without those servants, Dr Savage said, the heroine would not have been able to work. Her message to the young woman in the hall was, therefore, 'get good servants'. That's what she said.

Dr Savage's exhortations give a fair indication of the relationship which had been struck up, after twenty years of feminism, between the sisterhood and the working class. The lady sisters employed the poor; and didn't pay their taxes or their National Insurance contributions. (We won't hang around here on the extraordinary paradox that a

Victorian model of motherhood should be offered to young women as a perfect ideal in the Nineties. We won't go back into the painful confusions of Victorian children at the absence and coldness of their parents; the children's bewilderments, continuing far into adulthood, at being brought up by employed strangers; the grim consequences for boys and girls of imprisonment from infancy in single-sex schools. Let's not lean our minds too far in that direction: we might lose our balance.)

The young women who are recorded in Sheila Rowbotham's book complaining about household drudgery were not much different from the blue-stockinged girls who passed among the poor distributing soup and condoms before and after the First World War. Their 'connections' with the working class were negligible, theoretical, imagined, false. It was not long before the particularly Marxian impulses of this effort were abandoned (whatever happened to the Claimants' Union?). Broadly speaking, the effort had been reduced from a general purpose of the Women's Liberation movement to a very much smaller group of socialist feminists by about 1975.

The larger class of war-baby women mutely acknowledged, in their retirement from the struggle for sororal identification with working-class women, that they had more pressing interests of their own. Those interests were given increasingly active expression in such groups as Women in the Media, the Publishers' Publicity Circle, the National Union of Journalists, Women in Universities and in Medicine and in Law and in all the occupations which now lay open to them and which they sought, with unease and uncertainty, to enter. In all those fields, they chose to see the appointment of a woman as a victory for feminism over a recalcitrant male establishment. Any tardiness in promotion for a woman was seen as proceeding from the coils of repressive patriarchy. 'Positive discrimination' in the form of special treatment for women was required to ease the general ill of society which hampered their progress. By these means, the Marxian diktats became useful tools of advancement for ambitions and in occupations which Marx and Engels would have found no difficulty in naming 'bourgeois'. Reservations about 'transitional strata' hardly applied to the daughters of prosperous middle-class families who were themselves taking salaried employment in vital institutions of state and of commerce. By 1975, the girls were no longer crying at their easels but were, rather, plotting their next step on the ladder of advancement and counting the digits on their accumulating pension funds.

Meanwhile, they continued the search for secure connections with women beyond their immediate sororal class. Their most fruitful and promising course lay in historical revisionisms by which they might join their suffering and their aspirations with those very blue-stockings of the former generations. For all reasons of academic sympathy, personal identification and facility of appropriation, the feminist movement of the Seventies addressed itself actively to the past, offering a view of history which was modulated and governed by the patriarchal perspective. A flood of books, plays and television films were penned celebrating the earlier movements for women's emancipation; they were given rousing Eighth Route Army titles like Shoulder to Shoulder.

While the sisterhood was, itself, in a strangulating pother of division over the representation of women in Parliament (should they be seen to join the primary institution of 'male' power? was there not something intrinsically alien to feminine values of sisterly earth-loving in the routine business of passing acts in a chamber?), they found secure reassurance in the deeds and struggles of suffragettes and in the pantheon of free-love enthusiasts of the late nineteenth and earlier twentieth centuries.

The Pankhurst women, having been largely forgotten as figures of significance, were resurrected as lost leaders, along with Elizabeth Garrett Anderson, Marie Stopes, A. S. Neill and Vera Schmidt. The works and ruminations of Havelock Ellis, Bertrand and Dora Russell, Beatrice and Sidney Webb, George Bernard Shaw, Wilhelm Reich, Sigmund and Anna Freud and Jung enjoyed an immense new run on the printers' presses and became the focus of intense, revisionist discussion. An arena of legitimate academic interest was entered with illegitimate intentions, resulting in a pre-ordained and bastardised account of history. An essential element of industrialised and capitalistic history was largely excluded from the deliberations of the sisterhood.

Not seeing the supreme importance of contraceptive and abortion technology in their own revolutionised circumstances, the sisters did not see, did not allow, the transforming importance of contraceptive technology in earlier movements of female emancipation. They chose, as ever, to describe those movements as heroic uprisings of militant spirit, after centuries of crushing oppression. Where contraceptive technology was discussed in these retrospective accounts, it was given a negligible place. The sisterly riders of the purple sage found it far more appealing to gallop through the psychic underbrush of female anima and male libido which afforded them unlimited licence for imaginative discourse on the eternal qualities of male and female sexuality.

The chronology and synchronising of historical events supplied a much less exciting and less dramatic account of the movement of women out of the ghetto of domestic confinement and into a broader domain of equality in rights of property and citizenship with men. A sketch of that history can be drawn which matches, precisely, the technological development of methods of contraception and the history of women's 'emancipation'. Following the lines of this sketch, it might appear that the changes which were taken to be victories of emancipatory spirit among women were *all* conducive to the requirements of capitalism: that the long march of the left towards the identification of the class which would be the dissolution of all classes had simply resulted in the creation of a larger class of wage-slaves required by national and international markets.

Consider the coincidences. The Matrimonial Causes Act, the Married Women's Property Act and a bundle of Marriage Acts all became statutes during the mid-nineteenth century. This was the first period in which the labour force of men was inadequate to the demands of the industrial economy. It was the period during which reliable condoms were first introduced and began to be manufactured. It was also the period which saw the first flourishings of feminism.

The final extensions of women's suffrage in the decades around the First World War, promoted by active feminist movement, occurred at the same time as the introduction of the Dutch cap for women. Those last concessions of full voting rights also came during a period when the demand for women at work had increased to an unprecedented degree. When that demand slackened, during the slump years, feminism waned.

Forty years of feminist quiescence followed. Within five years, however, of the introduction of the Pill, the West was thrumming with the rhetoric of the new feminists. At the same time, the market economies of the West and the changes in the technologies of industrial production required and facilitated the inclusion of women, in large numbers, in the professional and semi-professional workforce.

Just coincidence? I don't think so. I think you could apply a classically Marxist interpretation, historically determinist, to this chronology and come out with a verity which remains secure: markets require, technologies supply. A general formulation on those lines would probably pass without argument among the Marxians of the sisterhood, so long as it was addressed to any economic and industrial field other than contraception and its determining role in sexual life. If you invited those sisters and their brothers in arms to apply that general proposition to the technologies of railroad transport, motor-car production, aviation, space and satellite, computer and combine-harvester, you would probably arouse not a murmur of opposition.

How come they have so conspicuously missed the application of this formulation in their considerations of 'the woman question'? How could academic scholars, trained minds, dialectical materialists, have been so limited in their approach to an industrial culture? How could they have been so uninterested in the dynamic connection between the industrial mass-production of condoms, Dutch caps, spermicidal creams and unguents, IUDs and contraceptive pills on the one hand, and the demands of the labour market on the other hand?

Search me.

The question has, to a degree, got me beat. It is a Gordian knot of historical perplexity which may require greater brain-power than mine to unravel or to penetrate. Perhaps it will be more readily comprehensible to future historians. My best shot at the question is to take aim, again, on the impulses which drew the Sixties generation, with their general political estrangement, to the orthodoxies of the old Left. The girls of the Sixties sisterhood were so thoroughly discountenanced by the changes which the contraceptive revolution introduced that they were incapable of seeing those changes even in the terms of classical Marxist dialectical materialism. The terrors which those changes induced went beyond the descriptive capacities of a historical method. They could be answered only by The Great Terror of the feminist Seventies and Eighties, in which Eros himself was perceived as a dancing demon presaging the death of the planet and men were to be described as The Other, incarnating and embodying that evil.

FIVE

The Great Terror

'Men's spirituality is very badly mangled ... Men don't have intuition or sensitivity ... Women have total mind. Men's minds are not true ... We must learn about men and their archetypes in order to put them back in their place – they are an aberration and out of control ... Men won't exist for much longer.'
(J. Higginbottom and M. Roy in Feminist Action 1, *1984)*

If we are indebted to Marx for the account of class relations which the feminists appropriated and misapplied, we owe to Freud the psychological drives and underpinnings of the sisterhood's violent and primitive pictures of men. The Great Terror of the feminist Seventies and Eighties, conceived in an egg of scrambled Marxian dogma, was fertilised by a darting pin-head of Freudian theory. Thank you, Karl; thanks, Sigmund: y'all come back now, you hear: anytime you have something helpful to add.

It is a nice paradox that Freud, who has been kicked, baited and trounced by the feminists for his penis-envy theory, should have provided them with the psychological bones from which they erected the figure of their bogyman; but there it is and there you are.

In *Civilization and its Discontents*, Freud extended the picture of humankind in society which he had drawn in *The Future of an Illusion*. Freud saw the human being commonly named 'man' as being at odds in any culture with his primal passions. He must always struggle to repress and to contain his most essential subconscious drives and needs; and he will be eternally divided by his own ambivalence. Human society, in Freud's account, provided an external framework of constraints and taboos by which primal man was kept in check; and, internally, man converted his repressed desires into guilts and anxieties. Without those constraints, man would naturally run amok in murder, rape and incest.

This account of a primal human nature chained by social niceties was not Freud's invention. His genius was to discern the conflict in a pattern of sub-conscious phenomena, including dreams and hysteria, thus delivering an account of the outer world in the workings of the individual's inner mind. It is to Freud, then, that we owe the principal debt for the slogan which has become endemic to our post-war age, that the personal is political. Thanks again, Sigmund.

Before it took this essentially secular and individualistic form of expression, the opposition and conflict between the individual's primal nature and the constraining demands of society had been the eternal and universal common stuff of myth, legend, superstition and religious feeling and organisation. That perceived conflict is fundamental to our understanding of ourselves and always has been. It is pre-historic. It goes back into the forests of central Europe, from which it was excavated by the Grimm brothers. It crosses the deserts of the Middle East and the steppes of Eurasia. It is common to Judaism, to Islam and to Christianity; it is detectable in Sikhdom, Hinduism and Buddhism. Where the Analects of Confucius give the character and describe the obligations of a gentleman, they presume that there is a division in man between the necessary precepts of social morality and his own base, primal urges:

Yen Yuan inquired what constituted a moral life.

Confucius answered, 'Renounce yourself and conform to the rites.

'If one could only', he went on to say, 'live a moral life, renouncing himself and conforming to the rites for one single day, the world would call him a moral character.'

In Freud's own time and throughout the previous 150 years, the imagined and perceived tension between primal human nature and the demands of social organisation had become most immediately and vividly taxing as a dynamic intellectual problem. The growth in European populations and the birth of the great industrial cities called for new theories of social organisation which could make sense of these unprecedented happenings and give them order. In less than 150 years, between 1700–1850, the earth had moved under the feet of European peoples, disrupting a pattern of ownership and authority which had been settled for the previous thousand years. Consider a few outward signs of that shift: no police forces worthy of the name existed before the great European cities came into being. Since everything the peasant owned he owed to his liege lord, the property rights of the masses were born with the industrial wage. Before the growth of the cities and the accumulation of capital through industrial production, social authority, rather than being centralised and codified, was vested in the hands of local chiefs and lairds, princes and nobles in their fiefdoms, who were united in theory only in their obedience to sovereign, Pope and God.

During and after the Industrial Revolution, new theories were called for, not only to express rights of property but also to explain the relationship of individuals to social order. New codes of moral understanding were needed so that people might comprehend revolutionary changes which many apprehended as being thrilling in their potential for personal liberation and which others felt to be terrifying, either because they lamented the collapse of traditional order or because they feared the power of the centralised state. Theories were supplied in abundance. Everybody had one, at least – from Hobbes to Burke, from Rousseau to Sorel. Running through them all was a common apprehension that, for better or for worse, essential human nature is at odds with social organisation. The Betterers included the Romantics, from Wordsworth to Emerson. The Worsers included Flaubert and Tolstoy and those other vast figures of nineteenth-century fiction whose essential view was that the individual would always be at odds with the machines of his society's organisation and would, most likely, be crushed by them.

Freud's contribution was to give the gloss of the most modern scientific and medical terminology to the ancient and dreadful unease, finding in it the Oedipal upheaval and the death urge which is at odds with Eros.

Freud never went along with the Bolsheviks and with their fellow-travellers who liked to think that 'the Soviet experiment' would remove aggressive behaviour from human society. He never believed, as they did, that aggression was created with property and would to removed with the abolition of property. 'One asks oneself uneasily', he wrote, 'what the Soviets will do after they have exterminated their bourgeois.'

Nonetheless, Freud's essential tools of special analysis and description in *Civilization and its Discontents* and elsewhere in his work were lifted directly into the map-rooms and the marching packs of the modern sub-Bolshevist sisterhood, along with the orders they swiped from classical Marxism. Freud's dismal conclusions and prognostications, conceived in 1928/9 and amply fitting for the years in which

Stalin finally took a grip on the Kremlin and Hitler's Nazi party surged towards victory in the Reichstag elections, have permeated and informed the attitudes of this century towards the apocalyptic capabilities of human beings. In our own age, Freud's despairing picture of those capabilities has been vested exclusively in men, manhood and masculinity.

In *Civilization and its Discontents*, Freud said: 'Men have now gone so far in the mastery of natural forces that with their help they could easily exterminate one another to the last man. They know this, hence a large part of their current unrest, their unhappiness, their mood of anxiety.'

Freud's sentiments and fears recur, in almost identical terms and words, throughout modern feminist writing. In the last twenty years, Germaine Greer alone must have written and published a hundred versions of those sentences of Freud's. In *The Slag Heap Erupts* (February 1970), in an early instance, she wrote:

> The only genetic superiority that men have is their capacity for violence, which in this age of preparation for total war has taken on an institutionalized form. We all need to be rescued from the computer-aimed nuclear phallus that kills without passion.

Throughout the feminist canon, an unchained Other, running amok with his priapic proddings and pokings, threatening the survival of the planet with his phallic imperatives and his imperious demands for cold meat-loaf, warmed slippers and accommodating vagina, was opposed by a feminine ideal. Men being not fully whole in mind (see the epigraph at the head of this chapter), they were necessarily unwholesome in body. The future survival of life itself depended on the confinement of the male's bursting powers of destruction and self-destruction; and the chains by which he might be restrained were the chains of theory which connected the sisterhood, sometimes seen (most weirdly) as chains of love.

I know this doesn't make sense; but it's not my fault. I'm not responsible for the theory; I'm just trying to lay it out.

Why should I bother my head with the effort when Germaine Greer did the job in the Introduction to *The Mad Woman's Underclothes*:

> Everything I learn reinforces my conviction that the only corrective to social inequality, cruelty and callousness is to be found in values which, if we cannot call them female, can be called sororal. They are the opposite of competitiveness, acquisitiveness and domination, and may be summed up by the word 'co-operation'. In the world of sisterhood, all deserve care and attention, including the very old, the very young, the imbecile and the outsider. The quality of daily life is what matters, the taste of the food on the table, the light in the room, the peace and wholeness of the moment. Perfect love casteth out fear. The only perfect love to be found on earth is not sexual love, which is riddled with hostility and insecurity, but the wordless commitment of families, which takes as its model mother-love. This is not to say that fathers have no place, for father-love, with its driving for self-improvement and discipline, is also essential to survival, but that uncorrected father-love, father-love as it were practised by both parents, is a way to annihilation.

What a monster! What stupendous ego in perverted reason. Within this passage can be found all the strands of madness which made up the body of hatred and aggression in The Great Terror and gave it impetus and power in Western

131

culture from 1970 to the present.

Since the passage is a *locus classicus*, its sentences should be dismantled in turn. At every turn, the reader should ask: is this true of my own experience? does Greer's picture match my own view of the outer world and does it square with the evidence which has come my way?

To begin: is it true to say that 'the only corrective to social inequality, cruelty and callousness' is to be found in 'sororal' values? Looking around our world, after a quarter of a century of militant sorority, do we see that 'social inequality, cruelty and callousness' have receded, diminished or disappeared?

I don't see it myself. If any single consequence can be discerned for Western societies in their drive towards greater economic competitiveness, acquisition and domination in the Eighties of Reagan and Thatcher, of Donald Trump and Rupert Murdoch, of 'Dallas' and 'Dynasty', of Joan Collins and Jane Fonda, it is the wider and deeper spread of inequality between rich and poor and a cruel and callous indifference among the privileged towards those who are underprivileged. That widening and deepening has been endorsed and supported by the efforts of a powerful group within the sisterhood – a group represented by many journalists, editors and broadcasters – who claimed that the acquisition by women of Gold Cards, stocks and bonds, mortgages, pensions, executive briefcases, offices, secretaries, business lunches and deals were marks of emancipatory triumph for the sisterhood and, indeed, for all women.

Radical and socialist feminists, deeply divided by this phenomenon of female aggression in commercial competition, have tried to make out that the figure of the woman in the business suit boasting about her toughness in negotiation just goes to show the adaptive powers of male-dominated capitalism – its powers of repatriation, you might say – in turning women into clones of men. We have seen how the same line of spurious reasoning has allowed them to say that Margaret Thatcher had to be more of a man than the men in order to become and remain Prime Minister (why, then, were her most loyal and devoted supporters to be found among women of all classes and ages throughout British society? Oh, I know: those poor cows with their unraised consciousness *really* wanted a strong man in office; so they got him in the figure of Mrs Thatcher. That must be it).

Away with this bullshit once and for all and for ever. Let's be having and standing not another moment of it.

The evident and incontestable truth is that very great numbers of women in the West have taken pleasure in commercial competition, in acquisition and in domination. They have not merely backed unwillingly into the roles and styles of commercial life, spurning perquisites and turning down a bigger company car. They have flung themselves into those roles and styles with abandon and gratification. They love that life, damn it. They may even – see Goldie Hawn's *Private Benjamin* – find the delights of sorority and the gratification of career ambition in military service.

A sorority, it appears, may take any form, share any interests, express any ambitions. In the essential nature of female societies there is nothing automatically kindly, caring or co-operative. Sororities form themselves out of groups of women who share particular interests; and they may well declare themselves to be opposed to other sororities – as the bands of Tory ladies and the Daughters of the American Revolution have regularly declared themselves, scathingly, opposed to feminist orthodoxies and decidedly in favour of capital and corporal punishment and other social policies which might be called cruel and callous.

If it is true that, 'in the world of sisterhood, all deserve care and attention, including the very old, the very young, the imbecile and the outsider', then we have to say that, for all its cultural dominance, its hectoring claims and its hold upon media industries, the sisterhood has failed miserably to make *its* world into *the* world. Nobody seems to be in much doubt that, in the 1990s, social provision for the very young, the very old, the imbecile and the outsider is in a very much worse state than it was twenty years ago. Meanwhile, it is obvious that women who are expected to work full-time cannot, simultaneously, be expected to offer care within their own households for the very young, the very old and the 'imbecile' (otherwise known as somebody suffering from a mental illness).

It is pea-brained cant to say that, if women were running the world, a better and more humane set of priorities would be established and care would be sympathetically provided for all who need it. As far as the administration of the social welfare institutions is concerned, women *have* a very big hand in running the world. They have been admitted to those institutions on equal terms with men for nearly a quarter of a century. Women have, for instance, been admitted to the medical and teaching professions in equal numbers with men for more than twenty years. Women do not occupy many of the top jobs in those professions, for reasons which I want to discuss further on, but it just won't wash any longer to say that the defects in those institutions and the poverty of the care they offer is the fault of men and of the patriarchal orders they impose. If the 'sororal' values were so patently superior – if indeed they existed at all – we should, by now, have seen some positive improvement in our social provisions for the needy. We have seen the reverse.

Passing over the puzzling notion that women might care more than men about the quality of daily life and 'the peace and wholeness of the moment' – a claim which might surprise the Benedictine no less than the country gardener, the angler, the painter, the photographer, the rambler and the cook — we come to the forms of perfect and imperfect love as they are divined by the all-seeing Doctor.

Here we are given such an exquisite formulation of the sororal totalitarianisms and terrors of our time that they might be inscribed on gold leaf and sealed in a time-capsule for the edification of the future world. Heterosexual love, in Dr Greer's psyche, may not be perfect because it must be riddled with hostility and insecurity. Father-love may not be perfect because it is selfish, in its drives both for improvement and discipline. Only mother-love, the model for the 'wordless commitment of families', offers the way to perfect love.

Seeing father-love as driving solely towards the improvement and discipline of the self, she must view father-love as a force which drives towards annihilation, both of the self, in its own death, and of the planet, in holocaust. Dr Greer does not know and cannot believe that father-love may be selfless. It is not in her universe to know that a father may find the rapture of pure joy in the birth and life of his children, knowing that their creation hastens the day of his own extinction and welcoming that vision. Even if the unfortunate Dr Greer has been deprived of this blessing by happenstance, it is still rather strange that somebody so erudite should not have caught a glimpse of it in literature. Some mighty big holes must exist in Dr Greer's education or in her powers of attentiveness and understanding if she cannot collect the vision of a selfless father-love from Jesus of Nazareth; or from Wordsworth; or from Darwin's notebooks on his child's infancy; or even from The Prophet of Kahlil Gabran, who said in *The Prophet*:

Your children are not your children.
They are the sons and daughters of Life's longing
for itself.

They come through you but not from you.
And though they are with you yet they belong
                                        not to you.

This vision was first published in 1926, exactly at the time
when Freud was composing his terrifying picture of the
anti-social Other which the sisterhood has found to be so
much more informative. Why the Freudian nightmare
should have been found to be so much more captivating and
engaging than the vision of love in Kahlil Gibran is another
of those enticing questions, inviting historical analysis, with
which future scholars may delight themselves: it is a
question of the same order of magnitude as the question why
the young of the Sixties turned in such numbers to the old
orthodoxy of Marxism in their distress over the deeds of the
political establishments of their day.

I can go no further than to affirm the essences of parricide,
of anti-Eros and of fear of the phallus in The Great Terror of
modern feminism. A simpler way to put this is to say that
they found it impossible to believe that all men might be
Jesus, William Wordsworth or Charles Darwin; and irresistible to believe that all men were and are Idi Amin; or
might want to be.

All the evils which Freud had described as being held in
check by social constraints and taboos were seen, by the
feminists, as being intrinsic to manhood and as being
practised on a vast and hitherto unrecognised scale. The
sisterhood turned, from its first gatherings, to the issues of
rape, domestic violence and incest, as it was apparently
discovered in the sexual abuse of children. From their
earliest utterances to the present day, the sisterhood has
claimed that these deviations were infinitely more widespread than 'male-dominated' society would recognise, that
the official figures were 'the tip of the iceberg' and that, in

their incidence, they denoted a true essence of masculinity. In other words, the sisterhood claimed to be able to see beyond the shadows of social organisation into the heart of primal man; and they discerned in that heart a profound and ghastly horror proceeding from the organ of generation itself.

Derision, sneering and jeering about the phallus and its potencies and failures has always been a singular feature of this psychical discernment. Feminists have been laughing about men's penises since before Yoko Ono announced that men had discovered humour in the wayward behaviour of the long thin thing which hung outside themselves and went up and down of its own accord. Like her, they have tended to see the penis as an instrument of its own independent will, separate from the person and the psychology of the individual man — a curious attitude to physiology in an intellectual movement which likes to think that its members see Nature as a whole.

Germaine Greer had a leading hand in urging on this sisterly derision, her authority supplying it with some measure of respectability. In *The Politics of Female Sexuality*, published in May 1970, she wrote about 'the male genital, the visible doodle, the tag of flesh that could become as hard as a fist . . . the tremulous dangling thing . . . his tassel . . . the pork sword'. Heterosexual intercourse she saw as an act of aggression, part of the purpose of which is the obliteration of female sexuality, 'the pummelling of one lump of meat by a harder lump of meat'.

In Dr Greer's mind, as in the sisterhood as a whole, it appears that some switches must have flipped between 1968–1970. At the earlier end of that brief period, she was an editor of *Suck*, an underground sex magazine published from Amsterdam. The covers and pages of that publication were adorned with photographs and drawings of erect penises in such profusion that the journal was a kind of phallic fanzine, glorying in potencies and extolling every cell of erective tissue. Germaine Greer contributed lip-smacking items to this journal, exhorting women to shed their inhibitions in the arousal of the organ and to take fuller measure of the pleasures it offered.

I don't suppose that Germaine Greer can have had more than a hundred followers in the wide world for the phallic oblations prescribed in *Suck* (and it may well be that domestic life is a less taxing enterprise for their lapse into desuetude); but the followers she acquired when she flipped her lid and turned the totem of desire into 'the pork sword' and 'the visible doodle' may be numbered in millions. Following Greer, the prick became a joke all across the West, the essence of humour discovered in male anatomy and described with distaste or disgust. Men, themselves, were pricks. Nothing more.

No feminist writer has taken up this attitude with more enthusiasm than Rosalind Miles nor carried it further into a realm of darkness wherein the phallus itself is the instrument which menaces the cosmos. Derision and disgust march hand in hand with terror throughout the pages of her book *The Rites of Man*. She quotes the views of one Esther Vilar and affirms, correctly, that Ms Vilar's mockery could be paralleled a thousand times in the writings of other women.

Ms Vilar wrote that when a woman first hears about the phenomenon of a male erection, the idea seems so absurd and grotesque that she cannot believe it happens. No theory, in her view, could be more ridiculous than Freud's theory of penis envy. Not even in the deepest reaches of her unconscious, Ms Vilar said, would a woman ever wish to be attached to a penis. That woman, she said, sees a man's genitals as being superfluous to the otherwise neat construction of his body. She cannot understand why a man is unable to withdraw his penis into his body and make it vanish, as if it were an aerial on a radio.

Rosalind Miles pursues this line of mystified disgust in saying that every man is in love with his penis. That love affair, she says, provides the true story of masculine sexuality. Let no woman put asunder those whom God hath joined at the root, she jeers, man and penis.

Men, themselves, have discovered and described this division between their moral selves and their penises since earliest times. The picture of a male spirit in hock to the imperatives of penile sinew has been, as Greer, Miles and those thousand other women have observed, a constant feature of the male universe since long before knightly and courtly romances expressed the division between the divine soul and the devilish flesh in the pure idolisation of the sainted lady who might not be defiled by touch. The hair shirt of Sir Thomas More was donned that he might draw nearer to Christ and God in the conquest of the flesh, as were the strictures of St Benedict and the longings of St Augustine. Since herding began, it has been customary among men to see the penis as the tool of Satan, the 'one-eyed trouser snake' whose urgings and temptations subverted reason and overwhelmed moral resolution – the serpent joining forces with Eve to destroy Adam. A thousand and one of the sisterly writers have quoted the Yiddish proverb which supports their picture of division: 'When the prick stands up, the brain lies buried in the ground.' Rosalind Miles quotes with pleasure from Paul Theroux's *My Secret History*, where he says, 'I had often looked at my penis and thought, "*You moron.*"'

The particular twist of the sisterhood was to turn those expressions of personal division into an account of eternal political verities, embracing all modern societies and accounting for all social evil. The personal being political, the sisterhood has treated those anguished or wry perceptions of division as indicating the essential and unalterable condition of man in the world. From a more generous – and one might say, holistic – point of view, the despair of men over the amoral promptings of the flesh might be seen as a profound psychical wound, proceeding from the incest taboo and from all forms of social organisation which preserved sure lines of paternity in the tribe. It is a picture of torment which might have invited sympathy and love from women. In our own time, however, in 1970 and thereafter, the class of Sixties women turned the hatchets of their psychobabble on the phallus.

Why should they have become so aggressive, so spiteful and so malignant in purpose, so intent on doing down the penis with derision and mockery, at precisely that moment? What made them so different from their forebears in all those human societies where female traditions honoured, praised, sometimes worshipped, the phallus, its generative powers and the mystery of its erection?

The reader will know, already, the answer in my mind.

The introduction of infallible contraception instantaneously vitiated the social harms which might be wrought by uncontrolled erectile tissue and the ejaculate of seed it projected. The issue of life and death was not automatically raised every time a penis stirred. A woman might accommodate a passing or pressing penis – any man's – without risking her own life in giving birth, without the abridgement of any taboo.

Simultaneously, the prospect arose that men, finding nothing threatening to social order or to life itself in their sexual organs and emissions, nothing to resist, no reason for shame, might heal the primaeval incest wound and make one with themselves. Modern technology had delivered the

140

means by which men might, for the first time in all of human history, be released from the ancient agony in the renunciation of the world, the flesh and the devil. Carnal knowledge and sexual love might itself be a path to divine revelation, as Nietzsche and D. H. Lawrence had urged that it should be. After the Sixties, the way to the bliss of that union of self and of selves was open for all men, in all their domestic and sexual arrangements, not just to a cohort of free-love enthusiasts and the unfortunate women who had to bear their progeny.

The reaction of the sisterhood to this prospect might be summarised as 'Not so fast, brother: where do you think you're going with that flower in your hair? Get back to the hell where you belong.'

The vision had no sooner entered the minds of men and the realms of actual possibility than it was attacked by the massed ranks of the sisterhood. From about 1970 onwards, the pseudo-Marxist claims of the sisterhood to see a means to universal emancipation through the class oppressions of women were steadily dropped from the movement's mainstream: they were replaced, with stunning rapidity, by a set of hostile denunciations which, in sum, declared that the phallus was the eternal root of all the evils of the world. Enter the spectres of rape, violence and incest, beheld in the sexual abuse of children.

WAR (Women Against Rape) was organised in the earliest years of the Seventies. One of its first declarations was 'Rape, like charity, begins at home'. This slogan, which enjoyed a measure of national popularity, matched the character of the sisterhood's most favoured slogans on the relationship between the outer world and the inner: superorganic ills were to be perceived and countered in a limited domestic theatre. In the case of rape, the ills of the outer world were not 'all inside your head, man' but 'all inside your vagina, woman'. According to their picture, heterosexual penetration was, itself, a species of invasion, of abuse and of the imposition of power. Rape was merely the naked impression of the brutalising instincts all men shared.

In *The Past is Before Us*, Sheila Rowbotham records and discusses this development with admirable decency and with evident unease. Noting the rapid facility with which the slogans on rape broke through another set of restraining points of reason and were applied indiscriminately to pornography, she wrote:

> The scope of coercive violence was extended. 'Pornography is the theory, rape is the practice.' 'Pornography is violence against women.' These made pithy slogans but they led to the conclusion that a physical violation was the same as an offending image or fantasy. This had extensive and alarming implications. It was linked to the assertion that heterosexuality was a form of control and thus inherently violent. The physical act of penetration was said to be necessarily oppressive. Anger against specific actions in which men violated women was magnified into an interpretation of social relations in which all men became simply 'the enemy'.

So it was, as a matter of recorded fact, in the writings of the sisters, from Germaine Greer in the earliest days to Andrea Dworkin and, in the present instant, Rosalind Miles. Rape became a synonym for sexual intercourse; the publication of erotic words or pictures, easily and readily described as pornography, became synonymous with the act of rape. The deviant sexual tastes and derangements of a very few men were magnified, without regard to evidence, as being common to every individual who shared their gender.

In *Sexual Violence: The Reality for Women*, composed by the London Rape Crisis Centre and published by The Women's Press in 1984, the authors described rape as being 'not an abnormal act but . . . part of the way men treat us as women'. It followed, in their minds, that no distinction could be made 'between "normal" men and rapists'. They acknowledged that men may opt not to rape but, they averred, all men are capable of the act and know themselves to be capable. These realities, as they described them, had been obscured, in their view, by a network of myths about rape and a silence about its incidence. Without that concurrence of myth and silence, they said, 'society as we know it could not function as it does'.

Other authors have claimed the support of statistical evidence to confirm the general asseveration that rape 'is not an abnormal act'. In a note at the end of her novel *Mercy*, Andrea Dworkin reports that a study of 930 'randomly selected adult women' conducted by the National Institute for Mental Health in San Francisco in 1978 had found that forty-four per cent of those women had endured a rape or an attempted rape at least once.

This study, according to Dworkin, was based upon the California State definitions of rape, which are: penile – vaginal penetration which has been secured by force; or by the threat of force; or intercourse completed when the woman was drugged, unconscious, asleep, or otherwise helpless and unable to consent.

The reader must ask him or herself: do I believe these claims? Is it possible that, effectively, one in every two women has been raped? That means that, if your mother has not been raped, your sister must have been. Or, alternatively, if none of the women in your circle of acquaintance has ever been raped, then it must follow that all the women in another circle must have been raped.

Even without knowing the 930 randomly selected adults in the San Francisco survey, even without sight of the specific terms of the questions they answered, we may reasonably guess that some generous extensions of definition have been effected to allow 44% of women to claim that they have been raped. If criminal rape includes a drowsy Sunday morning leg-over where neither partner is fully conscious and one of them may be wishing for a few more minutes of uninterrupted snoring, I suppose we may all, men and women, say that we have been rapists *and* victims. If criminal rape includes those occasions when both of the couples have taken on such a load of intoxicants that neither is fully capable of a clear-headed declaration of consent or refusal, yet intercourse is completed withal, we may all acknowledge some rueful degrees of guilt.

It does appear that some figures given for the incidence of rape must have been stretched by these means to obscure the specific qualities of a criminal rape and to include common acts and forms of behaviour. In the last months of 1991, extensive publicity was given in British newspapers and broadcast programmes to a survey emanating from Cambridge which claimed to show that one in five women had been raped. 'Today', BBC Radio's flagship current affairs programme, reported and discussed this claim as a fact as did many other media of news reporting. None of the reporting which I saw investigated the qualities and the statistical soundness of the survey. Nobody asked of the Cambridge women who presented this finding: 'How many women did you ask? Where did you find them? Who were they? Were you careful to include subjects in a wide variety of age-groups and economic classes? Did you make sure that your survey took account of regional variations and the differences between towns and cities?'

Having met some of the women who were responsible for

that survey, I can say that I am pretty sure that their results are worthless. Their method seems to have been to ask a narrowly selected group of young women whether or not they had ever submitted to an act of sexual congress without complete enthusiasm or resistless desire. Their results were published around the time that the trials of William Kennedy Smith and Mike Tyson were proceeding in America on charges of 'date rape'. The Cambridge women claimed that their investigations proved that the phenomenon of 'date rape' was, indeed, universal.

The single point of abiding interest in their survey is not its dubious method nor its incredible result but its evident purpose. The Cambridge women wished to show that all women – members of the abused and oppressed class – place themselves at risk of a violent violation when they enter into intimate connection with men, the imperialist oppressors. Throughout the last twenty-five years, when the phenomenon of rape has been near to the centre of the feminist cause and critique, this purpose has been plainly detectable. To achieve its end, it has been necessary for feminist authors to muddle and confuse a legal issue which is, in any case, extremely difficult to pin down and prosecute satisfactorily.

Rape must be considered an act of violent assault, or it is nothing. It must, presumably, involve the penetration of a woman by a man against her will. I suppose that, for the technical purposes of the law, the act must be completed in tumescence.

In the nature of that act, it must always be difficult for police and prosecutors to prepare and establish a finished case. Unless independent witnesses will testify to having observed the act in progress and consummation, the courts will always have to depend upon one individual's account against another's. Supporting evidence by way of medical examination or torn clothing or broken furniture, suggesting a struggle, may be inconclusive, even if it is available.

If a woman knows her assailant and has some kind of close personal connection with him, there must always be a question about her role and the extent of her responsibility in the alleged act, even if it can be established that the act occurred; and this doubt presents the police and courts with significant difficulties in discovering the truth. If the woman has gone out on a date with the man, he may argue that she has already consented to a form of connection which must, in its obvious and essential nature, declare a sexual interest. If she has accepted tokens of wooing – be they presents or flowers, dinners or packets of popcorn – he may feel that she is giving signs of approval of his sexual interest. If she has gone at night to his hotel room, kissed him, taken off some of her clothes and touched his erect penis, he may begin to feel that she feels some reciprocation of his interest.

For the courts to arrive at a dispassionate assessment of an allegation of rape in these circumstances *must* be practically impossible. Feminist rape lobbyists have seen the courts' difficulties as being part of a male conspiracy to deny the realities of life for women. They have maintained that, as a first step, the allegations of a woman complaining of rape must be believed. No woman, they have said, would make an allegation of rape, submitting to the indignity and the horror of the proceedings, without substantial reason and significant purpose. It should be noted that the same claim for automatic belief has been advanced for women who allege brutality in the home and for children who allege sexual abuse. Feminists have argued that complainants should always, as a first step, be believed.

It is apparent that, in the feminist account of rape, aspects of sexual and domestic life which are common to both men and women (and largely accepted by both as part of the hurly-burly of grapplings on the chaise-longue) have been taken to

146

typify political relations of power between men and women. With dependable reliability, Germaine Greer gave vent to her own quirky version of this damnation, decking it out with the instinctive mutilations of reason and the fashionable posturings which made her an unassailable flower of the sisterhood for all the scions who grafted their fears to her stem. In 1973, Greer wrote 'Seduction is a Four-letter Word', an essay about rape in which she said: 'Nevertheless, men do go to jail for rape, mostly black men, nearly all of them poor, and neither the judges nor the prosecuting attorneys are hampered in their dealings by the awareness that they are rapists too, only they have more sophisticated methods of compulsion.'

'Probably the commonest form of non-criminal rape', she said, 'is rape by fraud — by phony tenderness or false promises of an enduring relationship, for example.'

Phony tenderness? The false promise of an enduring relationship? Can these be 'the *notorious crime* of the whole society' for which Marx was searching? We are back in front of the easel in tears again.

Insincerity, failures of absolute candour or duplicity in sexual dealings, conscious or unconscious, deliberate or unintended, are not — we may think — the sole preserve of masculinity. They are — are they not? — an aspect of all flirtation and may be an essential concomitant of all wooing, male and female. If all the victims of phony tenderness or the false promise of an enduring relationship may be described as victims of rape, there can't be many sexually active adults of either sex alive in the West who have not found themselves, from time to time, on either or even, simultaneously, both the giving and the receiving ends of those 'non-criminal' acts.

Fantastic and grotesque as Dr Greer's claims were, the line which runs between her and the sisters at the London

Rape Crisis Centre has been received among the common wisdoms of our time and extended into the established institutions of our society. All heterosexual intercourse has been perceived as a form of rape and all heterosexual men have been described as rapists, not merely by the more obviously vexed and troubled sisters in the farthest margins of reason but, increasingly in recent years, by powerful figures, shapers of opinion and of law, in the mainstream of British and Western life.

The QC Helena Kennedy, speaking on television at the end of a documentary programme about rape shown in the spring of 1991, declared that the criminal act of rape expressed the feeling common to men that they had the right to impose their power upon women. The feminist criminologist Dr Susan S. M. Edwards has been retained by the Metropolitan Police as an authority on crimes of violence against women. She has conducted her research work with the active encouragement and help of police forces and she has given thanks to the Metropolitan Police and its Commissioner Sir Kenneth Newman 'for the sensitive and serious reception that the findings and recommendations of the [her] policing study have had'. The tenor of Dr Edwards' attitudes may be drawn from a passage of her book *Policing 'Domestic' Violence* published in 1989:

> Many laws mirror and reflect patriarchal privilege, and while the relationship between law and the patriarchal state is not implacable, laws regulating rape and assault against wives/cohabitees in the home mirror some of the worst excesses of the permission of male power and control over women.

This orthodoxy has become a tool of routine instruction in the education of the young. In *Feminist Politics and Human*

148

Nature by Alison Jaggar, a standard text in Womens' Studies courses in North American universities, you will read that, 'from prehistoric times to the present, rape has played a critical function. It is nothing more nor less than a conscious process of intimidation by which *all men* keep *all women* in a state of fear.' (Her italics.)

The moment has come in this discussion for a few questions to be aired.

If the crime of rape is so profoundly illustrative of the essence of sexual relationships between men and women, why – we must ask – is it committed so infrequently? If all men are capable of that criminal act and know it, why do few of them (us) commit it? Why, in the nearly thirty years of my active heterosexual life, have I never committed this act myself nor desired it? Why has none of my men friends ever confessed, in the privacy of those conversational intimacies which Dr Jonathan Miller cannot imagine, to the execution of the act of rape nor even admitted to a latent desire for it? Why have I only met two women in the last twenty-five years who claimed, themselves, to have been raped – one of whom was regarded, truly, by her own women friends as being unreliable in her accounts of herself?

For the last several years, I have been asking many people I met to tell me how many women they knew, for certain, to have been raped. I can't say how many people I might have asked; but I would guess it runs into some hundreds. In this haphazard and thoroughly undependable survey, the commonest response, by far, has been to say that the respondent has known one or two such women. Only one woman claimed to have known of five such incidents. Very many of the people I have asked, young and old, men and women, have said that they have never known a woman who was raped. I want to recommend that the reader should try this approach and test, within your own society, the various claims that

44% or, alternatively, one in five of women have been raped. I urge you not to keep the results to yourself.

Even if we allow that our own personal experience may be limited, even if we accept that the life of our circle of acquaintance may not represent the lives of other societies, even if we allow that significant numbers of rapes are not reported to the authorities (and I must say that the evidence for that claim appears, itself, to be largely anecdotal and not absolutely dependable), there remains an unbridgeable gulf of credibility between the claims of feminist rape lobbyists and the evidence of our own lives. What is the explanation for this discrepancy?

These questions are so infuriating to feminists that a man places himself in some danger by asking them. He can expect to be screamingly denounced as an agent of male oppression, denying the grim and terrible realities of life for women. No expression of reserve, doubt or scepticism is permissible on this subject. The storm of hysteria which envelops the subject may well be taken as a mark of the falsehood with which it has been wilfully endued by the sisterhood. They cannot permit a calm discussion of evidence because the evidence is so plainly contrary to their declared analysis and purposes.

Since this discussion is simply between you and me in the secure privacy of bound pages, let's ignore those menacing and hysterical rantings and try to take a few calm steps in the quiet groves of the facts.

In the records of the crime statistics published by the Home Office, sexual offences, as a whole, represent less than one per cent of all reported crime. Despite the threefold increase in its reporting in the last ten years, the crime of rape represents only ten per cent of that one per cent. If, therefore, crime is to be called, in the fashionable argot, 'deviancy', we can say that the crime of rape represent 0.1%

of all the criminal acts of deviancy in our present society.

If you look at the age-bands of victims of rape, it appears that women under the age of sixteen and over the age of thirty are, statistically speaking, at zero risk or rape. They are not much more likely to be raped than they are to be bitten by a mad dog and contract rabies. They are infinitely (I use the word carefully) more likely to be killed or maimed in a road traffic accident. If four-fifths of females are, statistically speaking, at no risk of rape it follows automatically that the crime of rape cannot express the experience of all women in their relations with men. If, even within the age-band of young women which contains almost all victims of rape, the chances of a woman being herself a victim of the crime are 1–2000 (being the number of criminal accusations averaged against the age-group as a whole), the incidence of the crime cannot be said to express the true relationship of all women in that group with all their men.

One in two thousand sounds like too much to be tolerated. If fifty women are raped for every 100,000 women in the population aged between sixteen and thirty, something deeply terrible is happening and it must be addressed. But even this figure is an exaggeration. The number of reported incidents of rape exceeds conviction in the courts by seven to one. This figure is given by members of the sisterhood such as Rosalind Miles to illustrate the pernicious procedures of a male-dominated legislature, judiciary and police force and it is offered to show the degree to which that establishment is unwilling to acknowledge women's special interests and experiences.

That is, assuredly, one way of looking at the figures. Before we look at them another way, let's not lose sight of the specific numbers, as they are given by Rosalind Miles herself. She says that almost 3000 rapes were reported in Britain in 1988. Just over 1000 went to court, resulting in only 420 convictions. Over 60% of rape victims know their attackers.'

So, if there are about 6,000,000 women in the United Kingdom aged between sixteen and thirty and there are about 420 – let's give it a generous round figure and call it 500 – convictions a year for rape, it follows that there is one proven criminal case of rape per year for every 12,000 of the women who are in the age-band wherein most rapes occur. If you apply the number of convictions to the female population as a whole (after all, we are supposed to be considering a manifestation of the notorious crime which illuminates the attitudes of all men, as a sex, to all women, as a sex), it turns out that there is one conviction for rape for, roughly speaking, every 60,000 females in the population.

You do know, don't you, what the sisterhood has to say about these figures? They say that the reported incidence of rape is 'only the tip of the iceberg'. They say that the police habitually report rapes as 'no crime' and that women are extensively discouraged, by social custom and taboo, from reporting and prosecuting offences of rape. That's what everybody says and thinks. In the last twenty years, I can't remember ever once hearing a contrary account of the rape figures: they are viewed from the standpoint of a uniform orthodoxy endorsed even by the police themselves.

That doesn't look to me as if it can be the whole story. I suspect that there may be another view of this picture.

The interests and specific difficulties of police forces in the West have coincided precisely with the claims of the sisterhood on the phenomenon of rape – and, indeed, of other criminal misdeeds in family, domestic and sexual life. The sisterhood has, by one interpretation, delivered into the hands of Western police forces a vital lifeline, without which their performances in combating and arresting crime would have seemed to be intolerably deficient and inadequate.

Rosalind Miles gives it as a fact that rape victims know their attackers in more than 60% of reported incidents of rape. Though we have already seen – and shall see again – that Dr Miles can be undependable with a fact or a figure, let's assume that, in this case, she knows what she is talking about and has got the percentage correct. It does not seem implausible that 60% of rape victims should know the identity of their attacker; if anything, you might expect the percentage to be a bit higher.

Now, ask yourself this: what other crime can you nominate for police investigation in which the victim knows and can name the perpetrator in at least six out of ten cases?

Mugging?

Burglary?

Robbery – armed or unarmed?

Autotheft (taking and driving a vehicle without the owner's consent)?

Theft from motor vehicles?

While crimes of these kinds have risen, in all Western countries, by doublings and treblings throughout the last twenty-five years, the rates of arrest and 'clear-up' in conviction and sentence achieved by police forces have plummeted. In every country in the industrialised West, it is broadly acknowledged that the police forces are largely powerless to protect the citizenry at large from the depredations of a very large tribe of criminal-minded young men. The task of the police in identifying and apprehending those kids who roll you in the street, or smash their way into your house while you are out at work, or slice their way into your car and lift your CD-player is, effectively, impossible. They haven't got a prayer; and, if you talk to coppers, you will find that they admit as much.

Desperate to feel collars, the police have made a meal out of domestic violence and sexual crime because it offers them

153

a manageable dish. They are much more likely to get 'a result' investigating acts of domestic violence and incidents of indecent assault or rape than they are to nail thieves and burglars.

By the same token, the police are far more likely to feel the collar of a husband whose wife denounces him as an aggressor than they are to catch muggers, burglars and joy-riders. Moreover, they will get heaps more public laurels for banging up the violent man than for bringing the muggers before the Juvenile Court for yet another wigging.

The apothegms of the sisterhood on rape and domestic violence have been a perfect gift to the police forces of the West. Their 'clear-up' rate in that seam of crime is the only badge of efficiency they can don, the only medal of achievement they can sport. No wonder the Metropolitan Police and its Commissioner give 'sensitive and serious' attention to the picture offered by feminist criminologists. It is one of the very few spars they may seize in a storm-tossed ocean of crime. They might welcome many more thousand reports of attempted rapes and domestic assaults. They would be profoundly grateful if we could be persuaded that sexual offences, in mass proliferation, truly express the criminal side of man in the world.

Even some of those people who are of a mind to endorse the sisterhood's claims on rape will admit that supportive evidence is negligible. I was recently arguing the toss on this subject with a Faculty Dean of a very large university who acknowledged that, in his twenty years at the same university, there had been some two or three rapes alleged. During that period, the total number of young women, aged eighteen to twenty-five, passing through that institution might have been 100,000. In the context of figures like those, rabies begins to look like a commonplace.

Some criminologists and sociologists have been moved by

the gulf between terror and reality in rape to say that if so very many women truly believe that rape is a real threat to their own safety, then the fear itself is a reality. In 1985, the British Crime Survey gave voice to a version of this pondering, saying:

> For rape, the BCS can say little, except that in comparison to crimes such as burglary, the risks of rape – and particularly of rape committed by strangers – are very low. This does not necessarily mean that 'women are worrying about nothing'. In general, one would expect rape to have a very serious effect on victims' lives – and there is nothing irrational about worrying about an occurrence which may be very unlikely to happen but is exceedingly distressing if it does.

The Islington Crime Survey, published in 1986, advances this position by a slippery step. Acknowledging 'the low number of actual rape or attempted rape cases' in its comprehensive account of crime in the borough, the ICS explained the fact that very many women were seriously worried about the threat of rape and sexual assault by saying 'although women worry more about crime happening to them than men, they may have a more realistic understanding of the probability of victimization than men do'.

What does this mean? Is there a real threat or isn't there? Do we see it or don't we?

I don't. I now believe that we have been chased up a totemic gum-tree by this rape terror. The whip has been cracked by those Marxian feminist criminologists who have made a decidedly uncomradely alliance with conservative 'law and order' lobbyists and with the police forces who are desperate in their need for publicity and promotional success. Those sororal comrades and the fraternal fellow-travellers who have hitched along should say fifty thousand Hail Rosas and make a pilgrimage of contrition on their hands and knees ten times from Trafalgar Square to Grosvenor Square, scourging themselves the while. They are a disgrace to every revolutionary young blood who ever spent an hour in Mayfair pushing and pulling with the bogeys and yelling 'class traitors' at the massed ranks of the men in blue. In all probability, the feminist criminologists of today who are so grateful to the police for the sensitive and serious reception of their work on sexual violence were themselves to be found in the ranks of those young bloods. Fie on them.

The rape fantasies of the sisterhood have never taken deep root in the social mind to the extent that they have significantly affected political policy and judicial practice. The extension of the law of rape to include acts committed within marriage is unlikely to result in a flood of cases in the courts. If reliable evidence to support prosecution is hard for the police to gather when rapes are committed in public places, their job is likely to be very much more perplexing when they are addressing acts between married people in their own homes.

Meanwhile, so very few men are arrested and brought to trial for rape that rape laws will always remain an issue in the margins of judicial practice. Violence between men and women in the home is, however, an issue on a very different dimension of legal, social and political practice: it can, with far greater apparent legitimacy, be held to be a routine feature of family life. Only by claiming that heterosexual intercourse is, per se, a species of rape could the sisterhood represent rape as a universal characteristic of dealings between men and women; and this claim has never cut much mustard, especially among those millions who find in heterosexual love a path – albeit a path more often blocked than clear – to delight or even to perfect and divine rapture in the communion of souls and the creation of life. A constant feature of feminist descriptions of 'sexual politics' is its outright denial of the longing for love in and between men and women and its decided declarations (see GG above) that love is not to be discovered between men and women in marital or domestic arrangements. This denial must be counted among the more signal perversions of modern feminism and the degree to which it has thwarted, frustrated or complicated the desires of men and women may be counted among its more pernicious effects. I shall have more to say on that point and others in the next chapter; but, first, I want to root around in the mess which the sisterhood has made over the issue of domestic violence.

Compared with rape, domestic violence has offered the sisterhood a very much more dramatically persuasive theatre in which to strut their stuff. Everybody knows and agrees that marital or extra-marital arguments between men and women often result in violence. Inflamed with passions gone wildly out of control, it is a subject tailor-made for magnification: a perfect instance in which the hysterical may be rendered political, in which primaeval terrors may be held to govern the orders of an advanced civilisation.

Domestic violence, like rape, has been the focus of a moral panic, fired by sociologists, criminologists and propagandists of the sisterhood and fuelled by the police and by ministers of state. The sisterhood stoked up this panic because, as they have claimed for twenty years, incidents of violence in the home illustrate the power relations of all men with all women and show us how far men will go to exert and keep control.

The *fons et origo* of those brutalising power relations

157

stands, they imagine, at the very axis of a man's being, in that mysterious, threatening and outward organ which – if it had any sense – ought to withdraw into the security of the body cavity, like a radio aerial.

As Rosalind Miles would have it, in *The Rites of Man*, the burden of fear of rape, from which every woman suffers, is the result of an understanding that the penis is inherently violent in its action. She sees it as the key to all agression – including wars, conquests, pogroms and raisings of ghettos.

All acts of *aggression*, then, return to the penis. The empire-builders, from Attila to Lord Curzon, have been driven by that mysterious outer Other and its promptings; and Mr Jones, the RSPB warden down the street, is following phallic orders in his domestic empire, enslaving the native freedom fighter within doors and enforcing his imperial diktats with the weapon of his 'pork sword'.

In 1971, the ever-loving Dr Greer gave voice to this view of violence, which the sisterhood subsequently shouted over the rooftops of every apartment house, terrace and bungalow estate in the developed world. In *The Female Eunuch*, she said:

> The male perversion of violence is an essential condition of the degradation of women. The penis is conceived as a weapon and its action upon women is understood to be somehow destructive and hurtful. It has become a gun and in English slang women cry when they want their mate to ejaculate, 'Shoot me! Shoot me!' Women cannot be liberated from their impotence by the gift of a gun . . .

In *The Female Eunuch*, Dr Greer did not have much time or patience for the claims of the women's movement that women were routinely subjected to acts of violence by their men. 'It is true', she wrote, 'that men use the threat of physical force, usually histrionically, to silence nagging wives: but it is almost always a sham. It is actually a game of nerves and can be turned aside fairly easily.'

Her interest in male violence was more keenly felt and displayed in an unseemly delectation for brawling scenes between men, viewed as a kind of spectator sport. She said, 'Violence has a fascination for most women; they act as spectators at fights, and dig the scenes of bloody violence in films. Women are always precipitating scenes of violence in pubs and dance-halls. Much goading of men is actually the female need for the thrill of violence.'

These sentiments are so profoundly and embarrassingly at odds with the feminist establishment in its declarations about male violence that it seems hardly fair to rake them up now, when the good lady doctor is well-advanced into her fifties, dressed in sensible skirts and shoes and peeping over scholarly demi-lunettes. Germaine Greer was, remember, only about thirty when she wrote *The Female Eunuch* and if she might have been thought old enough to know better but was, in fact, still susceptible to a flood of vaginal juices at the sight of one man grappling with another, the girlish pleasure ought to have remained a private thrill which might weary in maturer years.

The sisterhood has never, to my knowledge, given serious consideration to the idea that women enjoy provoking violence between men and observing the proceeding fisti-cuffs. They have given all of their attention to the general proposition that 'the male perversion of violence is an essential condition of the degradation of women'. From the first foundation of Chiswick Women's Aid, organised by Erin Pizzey in 1971 (now named Chiswick Family Rescue), the sisterhood has taken and declared the position that:

Battering is a social crime which cuts across all classes, religions and ethnic groups. The roots of domestic assault lie in social conditioning. It is society's responsibility to provide women with protection from abuse and to insist that the appropriate laws are enforced to prevent violence and not to condone it.[1]

The battered woman has become an icon of observance in the sisterhood and in the wider world whose terms of reference and consideration they have extensively determined. Nobody doubts that women are battered in enormous numbers; that the cases of wife-battering reported to the police are no more than 'the tip of the iceberg'; and that an essential feature of male/female relations is expressed in that plenitude of occasions when a husband or live-in lover takes his fists to his woman. (If I have one message for my patient reader, it is this: every time you hear the expression 'the tip of the iceberg' raise all the hackles of your scepticism and beware. Somebody is trying to have you on.)

The sisterhood has persuaded the wider world to see domestic violence as a function of patriarchy. They have asserted that men regularly, routinely, strike their women as a way to impose their oppressive powers; and that men have become more violent towards women as those patriarchal powers have diminished, following the triumphs of militant sisterhood. Dr Rosalind Miles, faithful as ever, gives the standard line of cant in *The Rites of Man*:

She says that men feel a greater need to exert and impose their dominance when they see that women are becoming independent and, thereby, usurping the patriarchal authority of the male. The means to reassert that authority,

---

[1] 'Key Principles' of *Chiswick Family Rescue 1990*.

she believes, lie in what she calls the weapons of sexual terrorism, a man's fists.

I want to attack, at root, all the presumptions and assumptions in this orthodoxy; but, before we go any further with this discussion, I had better allay some fears which must be rising in my reader's bosom. Your author is not about to claim that violence does not occur between men and women in their domestic lives. I am not going to say that blows are rarely or never directed and delivered in domestic arguments. Nor am I going to try to make out that women do not, as a rule, come off the worse in these encounters.

Take it easy, will you? There's nothing to get tense about. This is no more than a subject for consideration and argument, like any other. We're just going for another promenade through the thickets of recorded fact and statistic. Sure, it gets dark at times; but that just makes the shafting light in the woods more enchanting.

The figure of the battered woman rarely comes into Sheila Rowbotham's *The Past is Before Us*. Where she is introduced, Rowbotham assumes that the existence of a phenomenon of wife battering is recognised by universal consent and borne out by incontestable evidence. In her early pages, she says: 'The existence of coercive and brutal control was evident. The creation of refuges for battered women was an organisational innovation which enables this personal experience of subordination to find a social expression.' Towards the end of the book, where Sheila Rowbotham is reflecting on the increasing stridency of the sisterhood's damnations of men as they were heard towards the end of the Seventies, she says: 'The stress on violence was based partly on the grim realities revealed in the Rape Crisis centres and battered women's testimonies in the Women's Aid Centres.'

In the last twenty years, since Erin Pizzey first advertised the existence of the Chiswick Women's Aid refuge which she had founded, I cannot remember ever reading a single published line (other than a few I have written myself) in which any doubt or scepticism was aired about 'the [evident] existence of coercive and brutal control' or which questioned 'the grim realities'. We all swallowed every morsel of this dish of cant in a single sitting. The sisterhood was required to do nothing more than regularly load up the plates and keep us in a state of over-fed stupefaction.

So completely has the public absorbed the battered-woman image that it has become genuinely difficult to ask simple questions on the subject and receive sure and comprehensive answers. For instance, it seems almost impossible to establish with any degree of reliability how many cases of domestic violence are reported to the police in any year. You might expect that, in an advanced and computer-aided society, the collection and publication of that figure would be a matter of routine bureaucratic business. It is not. The Metropolitan Police reckon that they respond to 'about 25,000 calls a year' in cases of domestic violence. This figure is, said a spokesman who answered my telephone call, 'an extrapolation for London as a whole drawn from research in specific areas'.

That research, he said, had been conducted in the British Crime Survey, the Islington Crime Survey and in the work of Dr Susan S. M. Edwards, that same feminist criminologist whose work I have already touched upon. She is the one who wrote, in *Policing 'Domestic' Violence*: '. . . it is the precise juncture of bourgeois and male interest which constitutes the corner-stone of women's experience and corresponding oppression.' So we know where she is coming from.

The corner-stone of Dr Edwards' research is a work she conducted called *The London Policing Study*. With colleagues from the Polytechnic of Central London, Dr

Edwards studied the records of station messages received over six months at two divisional police stations, Hounslow and Holloway, in the Metropolitan Police District. It is not exactly clear from Dr Edwards' book what method of broader extrapolation she applied to the results of this research; but she does assert that: 'The number of women who officially reported violence to the police in the Metropolitan Police District alone in one year was estimated at 58,000.'

How did she arrive at that number? I may be wrong in this, but it looks as if Dr Edwards has simply taken the results of her research in those two police divisions and multiplied them by the number of divisions in the Metropolitan Police District as a whole. If I am wrong, the mistake is mine; but she has not been helpful in making her method obvious. If I am right, the extrapolation is worthless; and it proceeds from a statistical method so clumsy and amateur that it is surprising that its results should be given house-room by official bodies such as the police.

Think about it: are Hounslow and Holloway to be equated with Highgate, Finchley, Dulwich, Greenwich and Chiswick? Even if we assume that Dr Edwards has correctly gathered and assessed her research in Holloway and Hounslow – and, as she does not give her method, I am not in a position to judge – it would be simply preposterous if she had adduced from those specific figures a general picture of the incidence of domestic violence in Greater London as a whole. She would be making out that the differences between residents of those areas in income, employment, housing, racial tension and family structure made no difference to the frequency with which men and women living together get into violent rows.

Preposterous as the apparent method appears to have been, it has been endorsed by authorities sponsored with public funds. In 1986, the Police Monitoring and Research

Group published its Briefing Paper No. 1, entitled *Police Response to Domestic Violence*. Declaring that 'It is impossible to assess the police response statistically, because they keep no records specifically related to domestic disputes', the authors went on to hazard a broader picture of the incidence of domestic violence. They wrote:

> Dr Susan Edwards of the Polytechnic of Central London conducted research into police response at two London police stations, Hounslow and Holloway, in 1984 and 1985. Researchers found that over that period, the stations received between two and two and a half calls a day relating to domestic incidents. This would average out at over 1000 calls a week to the whole Metropolitan Police District.

Here we see, umistakably, that a suspect figure emerging from an undisclosed statistical method has been officially received and endorsed. It is, already, more than double the number which the police themselves report; and that police number has to be regarded with scepticism since the police themselves cannot account for it, except to say that it is drawn from research which we may guess to be Dr Edwards'. You will remember that the Metropolitan Police told me that they reckoned the figure for reported incidents of domestic violence on their patch was, on what basis they could not say, 25,000 a year.

We can only say that, for no good reason that can be ascertained, there is a discrepancy of 100% between the figure given by the Metropolitan Police and the figure which is supplied by an adviser to the Metropolitan Police. Somebody doesn't know what they're talking about.

We are about to receive another doubling, another magnification by 100%.

In 1990, the *Independent* published a column of mine in

which I questioned a policy newly inaugurated by Mr John Patten, Minister of State at the Home Office, promising to 'crack down' on violent men in the home. I suggested that the Home Office's figures had been bent to supply a false picture of domestic violence; and I hinted that Mr Patten might be taking a cheap political shot in the hope of attracting sorely needed women voters to the Conservative slot on the polling slip.

My article drew an angry reply from Sandra Horley, Director of the Chiswick Family Refuge. In her published letter to the editor of the *Independent*, asserting that 'abuse of women is a huge issue', she said 'The Metropolitan Police receive approximately 100,000 calls a year from women who are trying to escape male violence.'

We start with Susan Edwards' undependable figure of 25,000. We find it doubled by the Police Monitoring and Research Group, through the application of what appears to be an amateur statistical method. Now we find Sandra Horley, the country's most firmly established authority on woman- battering, saying that the figure is 100,000, and giving as her authority a speech made in the House of Commons by Chris Smith MP on 3 November 1986. Sandra Horley is a regular guest speaker on broadcast programmes, a constant subject for profile and feature writing in newspapers and magazines. On the subject of domestic violence, Sandra Horley is the national nonpareil. She is it.

Sandra Horley' figure of 100,000 calls to the Metropolitan Police reporting domestic disputes next went into the blender of Dr Rosalind Miles's intellectual stew, emerging as an indigestible knot of gristle in *The Rites of Man*. Dr Miles gives it as a fact that more than 100,000 women a year need hospital treatment after violence in the home in the London area alone.

Dr Miles does not give the source or authority for this

figure. The reader is entitled to wonder whether any such source or authority exists. We may wonder whether Dr Miles might have committed to print a fancy and a fiction which was likely to be questioned.

As with Dr Miles's assertions about men and their medical consultations for impotence, we may ask ourselves: 'How can it possibly be true that 100,000 women are treated in London hospitals every year for injuries sustained in domestic violence?'

If the population of the London area is, say, five millions, then two and a half millions are female. Of those two and a half millions about 750,000 will be in the age-range twenty to forty in which violent domestic altercations almost entirely occur. So, if 100,000 women a year require *hospital treatment* after violence in the home, that means that one in every seven and a half women is so badly hurt in domestic fights – bruised, contused, concussed, lacerated, burned or broken in bone – that they require treatment in, at least, the casualty out-patient's wards.

How can it possibly be true? How could the hospitals of London cope with such a demand? Ask yourself: how many women in all your life have you known to have required hospital treatment after a domestic fight? I know of one. One.

If, in the circles of my direct acquaintance and setting aside the particular enquiries I have made among doctors, magistrates and police officers on this subject, I have known one individual woman to require hospital treatment after violence in the home, it does not follow that women never require such treatment. It does follow that 100,000 women do not require that treatment in London hospitals every year. If one out of every seven women aged between twenty and forty received that treatment, I should have known plenty of them; and so should you.

You may think that this seam of argument is profitless

and redundant just as it is futile to ask 'Did Six Million Die?' about the Nazi policy of Jewish extermination. It doesn't matter if the figure was 5,857,652 or 7,354,693. What matters is that the Nazis executed their policy of extermination and that Jews were subjected to a genocidal attack and were murdered in millions. The overall reality is far more important than the specific number.

You may feel that the same argument can be applied to the issue of domestic violence: it doesn't matter exactly how many women are knocked about by their men; it doesn't matter whether the true figure is 25,000, 58,000 or 100,000; what matters is that we know it happens and it shouldn't.

I'm not so sure. What if systematic, routine and regular beating of a woman by a man is an uncommon, rather than a common, occurrence? What if there are no more than a few thousand (let's guess, ten) routine wife-beaters in the country? What if the perpetrators of that offence are often rather than unusually brought to book? What if the truth about domestic violence is not that the bigger and stronger partner simply belabours the weaker and more passive one but that domestic violence is mutual in shared aggression, if not equal in the injuries inflicted?

If any of this is true, the axioms of the sisterhood on domestic violence go for a burton.

It is obvious that plenty of couples get into fights and that women come off worse in these fights very much more often than men. The incontestable evidence may, indeed, be seen any night in any casualty ward of any general hospital and, if you want to see the evidence in all its sanguinary horror, drop in around midnight on Friday, our national night for fighting at home. I can even go along with the general proposition that some men like to hit their women and that some women feel unable to resist or to get away from those men, either because they are financially or emotionally

167

dependent on him, or both.

I have known three such couples in the last twenty years, three domestic menages in which the woman was quite often slapped and occasionally punched by her man. In each case, the woman was very young (under twenty-five). Each one of them regularly drank heavily with her man and one of them took drugs in very great amounts, often acting as the household supplier. In only one case that I know for sure were slaps and blows administered as part of the couple's sexual routines, as a prelude to or an accompaniment of coition: in that case, both the boy and the girl (they were very young) were dead weird. He was a regular subscriber to gay magazines which pictured acts of sodomy between men and gropings with animals. She genuinely seemed to feel that he was showing his love for her when he hit her. Different strokes, I suppose you must say.

None of these couples has lasted. Each individual is now living with somebody else. I don't know whether or not their new relationships involve violence: I would guess that they probably do.

These stories don't add up to a row of beans, still less a heap. They tell us that the ways of the flesh may be strange indeed and that declarations of love may be construed in acts which seem to announce its opposite. I tell the stories simply to show that I know and agree that there can be routine violence committed by men upon women. But I want to go further and say that what usually happens in domestic fights does not fit that classical stereotype. The general truth, I want to say, is messier and less schematic.

I want to draw from my own experience in sketching that picture. In cohabitations with four women over the last twenty-five years, including two marriages, I have four times been involved in rows which ended in blows. I have twice slapped a woman's face with my open hand.

The first time was when a woman from whom I had separated in scenes of nightmare conflict came to visit me in the friend's flat where I was temporarily staying. The whole of my right lower leg was in bandages and plaster, following a lacerating accident which had left me on crutches. My ex-lover was drunk when she arrived and got much drunker. We had a terrible row which was conducted, on my side, from the couch on which I was lying. In her rage, the woman took a picture from a wall (it was an Augustus John drawing) and tried to smash it over my leg, which was already held together by so many stitches that the surgeon who sewed them lost count. I was as angry for the friend who had lent me the flat and whose precious picture was going to be destroyed as I was for myself, feeling that my leg had been hurt enough. I slapped her face. She put the picture down.

I can't remember what the casus belli was in the second fight. The girlfriend with whom I was living was always a turbulent character and many were the storms and huffs between us. Whatever it was that got us going, I remember that we were rolling and tumbling on the bed – she trying to knee me in the nuts – when she yanked out a handful of my hair. I mean a complete fistful, a tonsure in a single tug. I slapped her. The fight stopped.

On the other two occasions, I was the one who got more badly hurt: my bleeding nose and lip and the deep scratches on my face were not matched by any injuries I inflicted in the fracas. In point of fact, I neither aimed nor landed a blow.

Drink was involved in at least three of the four scenes, as were hysteria, exhaustion and the kind of despair which comes over you in the middle of the night knowing that you might be in for a lifetime of marital misunderstanding and hostility exactly like the old folks at home.

Each of these unseemly and shocking incidents could be called a fight, though the word gives an impress of systematic pugilism to what were, in fact, farcical roughs and tumbles. Pains and injuries were inflicted both ways; mine were more gory than hers. There was, by any measure, an exchange of hostilities. The women were, beyond question, doing their utmost to hurt me. I can say, with absolute truthfulness, that I did not – never have – used more than a fraction of my strength or my power to injure; and, in two of the four scenes, I was using my strength to diminish injury. No medical treatment was required for any of the trivial injuries sustained by either combatant.

On each occasion, however, the woman acted as if her violence didn't count, as if the injuries and pains she had inflicted did not exist. I was made out to be the sole aggressor, named 'bastard' and 'batterer'. There was only one fell deed perceived in the mêlée and I was the sole perpetrator.

I want to suggest that a broader and more general picture of domestic violence may be drawn from these accounts (you may think this a form of extrapolation as partisan as Dr Edwards'; but, at least, my method is open). Where rows between men and women lead to fights, the violence is often two-way. Drink is often to be found in the picture. Injuries caused are very often slight and accidental.

These lines of approach are strengthened both by the visible evidence in the casualty wards and by the statistical records, such as they are. If you visit a hospital on a Friday night you will see men as well as women being brought in for treatment following domestic fights. The women may outnumber the men by, say, three to one; but the men's injuries tend to be more gruesome. Women's injuries are often the result of bare-handed blows from their men, so their faces and bodies get bruised, noses broken, ribs cracked or internal organs ruptured. Men's injuries commonly result from the use of some weapon; they are stabbed, slashed, scalded and whacked with every domestic implement that comes to hand, from the carving knife to the cast-iron saucepan and its boiling contents (or the Augustus John drawing).

How many of those injuries, inflicted by women upon men, are recorded by the police or any other civic authority? How many of them are included in any general discussion of the issue of domestic violence?

We have all endorsed the proposition that crimes of domestic violence upon women are one of the dark secrets of our national way of domestic life. The feminist campaigners have insistently claimed that women are unwilling to report these crimes because they do not want to embarrass their men and because their complaints are unsympathetically received and treated by the police and the courts. We have — haven't we? – all bought that line.

Try turning it on its head: see it from the other side. If women are unwilling to report domestic violence, how much *less* likely is it that a man might report injuries inflicted upon him in a domestic fracas? Is it probable that a man might complain to his friends that he got his head cracked, his nose broken or his ear slashed in a fight with his wife? Is it probable that those friends might say: 'You don't have to stand for that, you know. Get right down to the Crisis Centre and file an official complaint.'

Can you imagine that the desk sergeant would be able to keep a straight face while he filled out the charge sheet?

And yet, and yet . . .

In the face of all that improbability, it appears that one in four of serious injuries which are recorded as having resulted from domestic fights is inflicted by women upon men.

Let's go one or two steps further. Let's take a look at some of the recorded evidence which is available. In my view, the figures all suggest that there is not nearly so much serious injury committed in domestic life as the sisterhood has constantly claimed.

In its Briefing Paper No. 1, the Police Monitoring and Research Group gives the results of 'a specially commissioned analysis of the serious assault figures in England and Wales in 1984'. They record that 'Only 360 out of 19,002 serious assaults were recorded between spouses.'

These figures suggest that the issue of domestic violence has been comprehensively blown-up for polemical purposes. The murder statistics tell the same story, even more graphically.

When Mr John Patten launched his crack-down initiative against violent men at home, the Home Office supported the policy by reminding the public that 44% of all women who are murdered are killed by their husband or the man they are living with. This sounds like an unspeakably hideous fact if you give it only glancing attention, conjuring into the imagination a Sweeney Todd vision of mutilation and mayhem. It seems, of itself, to condemn men as homicidal animals who need to be chained down if they are not to be locked up.

If, however, you take the forceps and braces of a surgical scepticism to that figure, a truth emerges which is both less and more than the artful Home Office publicist had intended.

How many females would you guess are murdered in a year? The answer from the Mortality Statistics for England and Wales in 1987 is 147 (it was an average year). For women between the ages sixteen and forty, the figure – precisely 44% of the total – is sixty-five.

Sixty-five women were murdered by their husbands or lovers.

What do you say? What do you think? Does that number strike you as being so alarming that it should call for 'a revolution in the way that police deal with domestic violence', as Mr Patten described his initiative?

If you run your eye over the Mortality Statistics you will

see that 216 females died in 1987 from choking on their food; 305 died from falling on the stairs; 124 died of 'excessive cold'. If you keep on looking, you will see that, in the same year, 1435 women were killed in road traffic accidents and 20,000 women died from respiratory ailments connected with smoking.

Now I ask you: in the context of those figures, do you feel that a perfectly appropriate sense of judicious balance is being brought to bear on the sixty-five women who were murdered by their men? If you answer 'Yes, most certainly: their fate is the ghastly proof that men brutalise women' then you must answer a further question: why does nobody give a toss about the men who are murdered by their wives or lovers?

About 9% of all murders of males in any year are committed by their spouses. That makes about twenty murders of men in England and Wales. The number, like the number of women murdered, is reassuringly small; but if you want to say that the murder of women by their men exemplifies some kind of grand political scheme and dramatises the routine business of violence at every domestic hearth, then you have to admit that the deaths of those men complicate the picture.

The killer blow with which the sisters and their followers at foot always try to finish and to extinguish argument on domestic violence is to say that every women's refuge in this country is filled to overflowing. This fact, in and of itself, seems to be so imposing that it might silence sceptical questioning, requiring contrition as the only decent response; but, again, if you can get off the floor and look into the numbers, you discover another view.

How many women would you guess are being housed in refuges throughout the country at any one time? Thousands? Tens of thousands?

*not nos
changes
(230)*

I got the answer from the National Women's Aid Federation. They say that there are 'approximately' 160 groups offering places of refuge in England. The sizes of those refuges vary but 'the average number of places they might offer would be from six to eight'. Let's say the number is eight. That would make a total of 1280 places of sanctuary for women *and their children* in England.

Two-thirds of those 1280 might be children. Let's say that half the number is made up of children and the other half of the women who are desperate to get away from violent men. That would leave 640 women.

How can it have happened that a social phenomenon which results in 650 women and their children seeking refuge and care should have commanded massive and continuous, highly emotional and accusatory coverage? What the hell has happened to us as a generation, a nation, a people, that – in our damnable fixation with the proposition that the personal is political – the plight of 650 women should be treated with so very much more sympathy and political energy than, say, the million or more people who have, or may have, no home?

My answer to this question follows, in full, in a moment. I count this extraordinary discrepancy in sympathy and ineptitude in political practice among the cardinal failures of feminism and of the style of politics feminism has promoted. My subject, for the moment, remains the sub-Freudian terror of the phallus and of Eros which gave motive power to The Great Terror of the sisterhood. The last manifestation of that terror which I want to consider is the sexual abuse of children.

I have less to say on this subject, partly because the evidence is so thoroughly unreliable and partly because my thoughts are not yet finished and complete. For the moment, I would just like to air the doubts and uncertainties which are on my mind.

I happened to be close to the spot when the panic about the sexual abuse of children got started. In the summer of 1984, I went to Los Angeles for the opening of the Olympic Games and, while I was there, I looked into a story which I had heard rumoured in England. In Manhattan Beach, a prosperous Los Angeles suburb, it was said that children attending a Pre-School (nursery school) had been abominably abused by the staff and proprietors. It was alleged that they had been raped and sodomised in dozens; that they had been photographed and filmed for pornographic delectation; that animals had been tortured and killed before their eyes to let them see what would happen to them if they told their parents about their own ordeals.

In Los Angeles in the summer of 1984, the McMartin Pre-School scandal was the biggest of all stories. The public fixation with the alleged happenings in Manhattan Beach vastly exceeded their interest in the changes in the Soviet Union following the death of Andropov. Only the Olympics themselves were big enough to distract the minds of Californians and of all America from the horror which had been unearthed from the ground under their feet.

The McMartin scare was a real beezer. The nation caught fire. A score of arrests on similar charges were made in schools and children's societies from East to West. The darkest of all secrets had been told: adult sexuality was so perverse and uncontainable in its demands that grown people, most particularly men, would violate the bodies of infants.

Little children across the country were visited in their schools by counsellors who taught them a song about the difference between 'the good touch' and 'the bad touch'. Newspapers and magazines in America and in Britain ran thousands of articles under headlines such as 'Men: how can they do it?' (I'm not inventing that one). Fathers in their beds

175

on Sunday morning felt nervous when their own children snuggled under the duvet, lest a touch be misinterpreted. For the rest of the Eighties – and still today, I believe – a divorcing mother had only to breath the words 'sexual abuse of children' for the court to strip her husband of all his possessions, income and rights. The scare had the country by the throat.

The McMartin Pre-School trial was the longest in the entire history of American jurisprudence: the proceedings as a whole lasted five years. None of the defendants was convicted. Every one of them was acquitted. The jury broadly believed the prosecution's case – they felt that *something* evil had been done in Manhattan Beach – but they found the evidence insubstantial and insufficient to warrant conviction. That sense of something evil in the hearts and organs of men survived.

Britain lagged some years behind America in finding a taste for the horror of sexual abuse of children. The article I wrote in 1984 about the McMartin story and the panic it had inspired was 'spiked' by the then editor of *The Times* on the grounds, I was informed, that the allegations in the case were too disgusting to be printed in a family newspaper (I remember asking how an editor would apply this principle to the deeds of Idi Amin). Within three years, *The Times* and every other family newspaper were carrying banner headlines and full-page investigations into the nationwide phenomenon of child rape, buggery and molestation. No detail was then felt to be too disgusting for the nation's stomach.

Following the allegations of mass abuse in Cleveland and the setting up of ChildLine, the country surrendered to the awful sense that a horrible perversion was a common aspect of family life. Respected agony aunts such as Claire Rayner solemnly averred that we had come face to face with the last

176

great secret of our domestic arrangements, the skeleton in the cupboard which we had been unwilling to acknowledge. She said that her postbag regularly bulged with anguished allegations made by adults about their own childhood and by desperate children themselves. ChildLine has constantly claimed that 10,000 calls a day are made to its emergency telephone lines.

The Report of Lord Justice Butler-Sloss into child abuse in Cleveland does not make clear declarations in its conclusions as to whether or not the 121 children diagnosed by Drs Higgs and Wyatt as having been sexually abused were, in fact, so abused. The reader of the Report who must be intensely curious on this point is left to read between the lines of paragraph thirteen of the Final Conclusions, which says:

> Most of the 121 children diagnosed . . . were separated from their home, 70% by place of safety orders. The majority have now returned home, some with all proceedings dismissed, others on conditions of medical examinations and supervision orders. A few children went to one parent or a different parent and a few children were committed to the care of the council.

That's it. That's all the Lord Justice has to say. If we want to know 'Were those children buggered or were they not?' we can only reach towards an answer in the fact that most of them have been allowed to go home and most criminal proceedings against the parents were dropped. Which would seem to suggest – would it not? – that the children were not buggered or raped.

Lord Justice Butler-Sloss shows a similar caution, bordering upon incuriosity, in her general approach to the phenomenon of child abuse in the wider society. She clearly accepts that the phenomenon exists; but she is at a loss to know how extensive it might be. She wrote, in *Report of the Inquiry into Child Abuse in Cleveland* (1987):

> It has been impossible from the evidence presented to the Inquiry to arrive at any consensus or to obtain any reliable figures of the general prevalence of sexual abuse of children in the country or in Cleveland. Most data refer to allegations of abuse, or events in the protecting process, e.g. the number on the child abuse register ... The data show that increasing numbers each year are being investigated because of the possibility of child sexual abuse and increasing numbers of adults are complaining that they were abused in childhood ... We are strongly of the opinion that great caution should be exercised at the present time in accepting percentages as to the prevalence and incidence of sexual abuse. We received from published articles and oral evidence figures of 5%, 10% and upwards. Such figures depend on what is meant by sexual abuse. Some people have used the figure of 10% for serious sexual abuse, but there was before the Inquiry no evidence to support it.

I sympathise with the Lord Justice. I share her uncertainty. When respected experts say that they are convinced, on the basis of their own professional work, that sexual abuse of children is a widespread phenomenon, no citizen should ignore or underestimate their claims. I am impressed by a GP I know, also a sex therapist, who says that large numbers of her patients credibly claim to have been abused in their own childhood.

Against those claims must be placed the failure of social services and the police to obtain convictions in many of the major cases which they have launched. The fiascos in

Orkney and elsewhere, in which 'satanic' abuse conducted in 'rings' was alleged, deepen the suspicion in my mind that a panic out of all proportion to the dimensions of the phenomenon has got hold of the public mind. That suspicion took root in my mind in Los Angeles in 1984 and it has never been displaced by evidence. Does the sexual abuse of children happen on a large scale or does it not? I'm not sure. I suspect that it does not.

We have to suspend judgement, I think, on this question. We can be certain, however, about the propaganda uses made by the sisterhood of the spread of the panic. They *loved* it. They took it as a perfect gift.

The sisterhood had always claimed that men routinely violated children, that abominable acts proceeded naturally from the phallic imperatives. In an issue of *Shrew* in 1973, a contributor asked 'Are Fathers Really Necessary?' and concluded, as Sheila Rowbotham records in *The Past is Before Us*, 'that they were more trouble that they were worth and likely to abuse children sexually'.

Dr Rosalind Miles does not, so far as I can see, include the findings of the Butler-Sloss Report in *The Rites of Man*, even though the report was published in 1988, three years before her book. Perhaps she was unaware of the Lord Justice's reservations about the evidence for child abuse and her urging that we should all be very careful to know what we are talking about on this subject. Perhaps, also, Dr Miles was unaware when she was writing that the National Society for the Prevention of Cruelty to Children was riven with dissent over the Society's findings and policies on the subject. Nothing daunted, she renews her attack upon the phallus brandishing a cross of holy writ and a sheaf of questionable figures:

Repeating the words of Jesus, 'Suffer the little children', Dr Miles affirms that they do. She quotes figures published by the National Society for the Prevention of Cruelty to Children, showing that in the UK allegations of child sex abuse rose by 24% in 1989. She claims that 95% of those allegations were later corroborated. In the last five years, she says, certified cases of child sex abuse have doubled. She goes on to report that a 1989 survey by the Department of Health showed that one in four children had been abused, sexually or physically, or both.

I am not going to waste my time checking out these claims and allegations. If you are moved by curiosity, you might like to make a few inquiries yourself. See if you can find out whether or not she is right to say that '95 per cent of the allegations were later found to be true'. Try asking the Department of Health what, exactly, it means to say that one in four children have been abused. Does this mean that one in four children have been slapped by their parents, mother or father (if so, which)? Or does it mean that one in four children has been subject to sexual abuse by the father, requiring the service of his penis in one or more of his child's bodily orifices?

Over to you.

Meanwhile, let me come to the final point of this chapter, delving to the bottom of the pit of intellectual totalitarianism to which The Great Terror has sunk the sisterhood: here we find their claim that the evil of manhood and masculinity inheres in genetic and chromosomatic inferiority.

You don't believe, do you, that they have ever said that? You can't believe that any literate person who has received the benefits of a liberal education in the West could seriously propose – post-Auschwitz, post-Dr Mengele – that genetic defects and chromosomatic deficiencies might be the common characteristic of an entire division of humans who have nothing in common but their natural birth.

180

Brace yourself, therefore, to receive the thoughts of Dr Miles – and, therefore, to a degree of the sisterhood – on the biological inferiority of the male.

The essential and eternal human form, she says, is that of the female. Relying on the evidence of one Andy Metcalf that every zygote is feminine at the instant of conception, designated XX in chromosome, she sees the introduction of Y chromosome, designating masculinity in the foetus, as signifying genetic weakness. The strength which women derive automatically from their second X can never be matched, for men, by their Y.

From Dr Miles's point of view, therefore, masculinity is a form of genetic mutation. In that view, the male embryo has to break itself away from its essential female state to take up the alien condition of masculinity. She goes on to quote Dr Stephen Wachtel of the Memorial Sloan-Kettering Cancer Center, New York, as saying: 'You can think of maleness as a type of birth defect.'

Pressing further into this death-camp colloquy, Dr Miles, Fellow of the Royal Society of Arts, ponders some questions which might, with other applications, have been tossed around the mess dining-tables of Ravensbruck. She wonders if men may be doomed from the moment of their birth to struggle against the paucity of their genetic make up, with their natural aggression as their only weapon. Quoting a biologist, she describes their heritage as being 'the inadequate Y', 'small and twisted . . . a genetic error', 'a deformed and broken X', 'the shape of a comma, the merest remnant, a sad-looking affair' of the smallest relevance in 'organismal development'. Is the violence of men the vengeance they seek for 'the natural superiority of women' which biologists, Dr Miles says, have established.

Those biologists whose opinions and whose scholarship you may be tempted to honour (after all, how could anybody with a doctorate be other than honourable?) are one man. His name is Ashley Montague. In 1953, he published a book named *The Natural Superiority of Women*, which was based upon articles he had published as early as 1945. All the remarks about the Y chromosome in that passage of Rosalind Miles's are drawn from Ashley Montague's book. Not 'biologists' but one fruitcake.

That book is here with me on the table, as I am writing. I bought it in 1990 from The Sisterhood Bookstore on Westwood Boulevard in Los Angeles, in a paperback edition published by Collier Books. Ashley Montague is, the back-page advertisement says, 'a noted anthropologist and social biologist'. He is a Doctor. The blurb says that the book shows that the *'superiority of women is a biological fact'* and that 'women are emotionally and constitutionally stronger than men, quicker to respond to stimuli, better on IQ tests, less inclined to alcoholism and suicide'.

Hovering over the new feminism of the last twenty years has always been a toxic cloud of hokum about genetic predestination; and, in our time, the hunt for scientifically provable differences in physiology or gene structure between men and women has been more desperate than the long-lost hunt for physiological characteristics which might separate the races and prove that black people were inferior to whites by birth.

Without the desires of the sisterhood for scientific substantiation of The Great Terror, Ashley Montague's book about the genetic superiority of women might have become a curio in the bibliography of fascist ideology, along with the *Encyclopaedia Britannica* of 1929, which declared the natural superiority of white peoples. As the ideology of the sisterhood has developed over the last quarter of a century, Ashley Montague's lines of thought have been received into a genuinely influential body of opinion. There now exists a substantial library of writings which assert categorical differences in gene-structure, brain formation and essential, natural composition between men and women, invariably to the detriment of the male.

Among the more recent flourishes of this movement has been the publication in 1989 of a book called *Brain Sex* by Anne Moir and David Jessel. The authors promised to reveal 'the *real* difference' between men and women. That difference is, they say, that male and female brains work differently from the womb because they are doused there with different hormones. It follows that boys and girls come into the world 'with their minds made up'.

Moir and Jessel follow this argument through a maze of jiggery-pokery about the left-brain and the right-brain which originated, as far as I know, in some research labs in Stanford, California, in the Seventies and has since entered the main-course conversation of every dining table in the West, between the appetiser of Aids and the digestif of astrology.

If you have been spared this tomfoolery, you may wish to be left in ignorance; but a good summary can be taken from a review of *Brain Sex* by Wendy Steiner, published in the *London Review of Books*. She summarised the authors' propositions, saying:

> As a result of their neural structuring, men have an inborn advantage in mathematics, physics, abstract thinking, and all sports requiring hand – eye coordination. Compartmentalising their various mental states, they have difficulty expressing (right-brain) emotions in (left-brain) language. Most comfortable in object-relations and naturally aggressive, men are promiscuous, competitive and less emotional than women. Women's linguistic acuity, sensory

183

receptivity, and the extensive interconnection among their brain functions allow them to synthesise more information than men – the famous 'women's intuition'. They show an aptitude for all activities involving inter-personal relations (mothering, teaching, nursing). People orientated, sensitive and emotional, they are generally monogamous, and sacrifice prestige and gain for social cohesion.

The task of dismantling this passage is simply too wearisome to contemplate. We had enough of that in Chapter One. You must be familiar with the technique by now. I leave the passage and *Brain Sex* in your judgement.

SIX

The Failures of Feminism: Personal and Political

From the earliest days when they first donned the hood, some of the sisters entertained fantasies of the elimination of men, the extinction of the crippled, deformed and mutant sub-species. Few (but some) went as far as Valerie Solanas, who thought that men should, simply, be rubbed out. From the late Sixties, however, it was acceptable for sisterly writers to give the opinion that masculinity was redundant, superfluous and extraneous to nature, in the female whole.

Shulamith Firestone's book *The Dialectic of Sex: The Case for Feminist Revolution* conjured into vision a picture of a man-less society in the near and attainable future. Harping on the near-fact that an ovum might be fertilised by electrical charge rather than by sperm and that gender might be determined by science rather than being abandoned to the chance of chromosomatic collision, she exulted in the women's liberation which these technological changes offered. Women, she foresaw, might become pregnant without coition and insemination, through the implant of ovae fertilised in lab cultures. Life might be reproduced and gestation completed entirely outside the womb. Thus women might choose to eliminate the male from birth and from the earth. Through parthenogenesis, sisterhood would rule, unchallenged in supreme autocracy.

This vision scared me near to death in a Woody Allen-like panic attack when I first read it, as a 24-year-old in

1971. I had, I realised, been born into a doomed species and was, myself, useless to creation. It took me about five weeks to shake off the suicidal depression which followed from that reading. The moment of release came when I realised that if masculinity was removed from nature, it must follow that femininity would itself be redundant and would be eliminated. Femaleness is, obviously, a state of Nature which exists only in relation to its compatible opposite. No male: therefore, no female.

You may think that I must have the wits of a brontosaurus if it took me five weeks to see through that yawning flaw in Shulamith Firestone's logic (where were you when I needed you twenty years ago?). I can only answer that others have not seen the fault yet and remain enthusiastic for the final triumph of the female in the redundancy of the male. Seriously.

Firestone had been driven from the tears she shed in front of the easel over the waywardness of men towards a techno-dream vision of machine-made life which excluded the penis and its scrotal works. Her Frankensteinian passions caught the imaginations of other young women of the age who, evidently, were not easy with the receiving of seed, the conception of life and the delivery of babies from their own wombs. One of these young women is quoted by Sheila Rowbotham in *The Past is Before Us*, saying,

> . . . we will not be able to achieve full emancipation of the potential of both sexes without taking on the question of reproduction, and I mean that in the most basic sense of having babies. For all the discussion about why men and women lead such different lives today takes for granted the basic difference between men and women: that women are potential child-bearers while men are not. Visions of a future society

186

have to take this into account, whether it be by eradicating this difference, as Shulamith Firestone suggested, or ... by abolishing the social division between productive and reproductive labour.

When Shulamith Firestone was writing, the vision of supererogatory masculinity, of a sub-species which would wither away by natural selection, was far-out and shared only by a limited group of conspicuously weird and troubled sisters. In the last twenty years, the vision has acquired some measures of respectable orthodoxy.

You may recall from the first chapter in this book the name of Jane McLoughlin, author of *The Democratic Revolution*, who predicted that, in future, women would wear men as fashion accessories, like an alligator handbag. You may have supposed that she was joking. The sense of humour was macabre, you might have thought (and a touch unfriendly towards alligators), but, plainly, nobody could seriously harbour such a notion.

Think again: this is what Jane McLoughlin has to say:

> One of the anthropological pleasures of the 1990s will be watching how men cope with a new role – that of the redundant male. New technology will wipe out their traditional advantages at work, favouring as it does female skills based on dexterity, not strength. An influx of skilled mature women into the workforce will erode the self-protective isolation on which men have built their authority. More than a quarter of live births are outside marriage, marginalising the father in the family; he will no longer automatically be the only, nor even the main, breadwinner. As a final nail in the male coffin by the mid-1990s it will be simple for single women who want children to become pregnant through artificial insemination. This is

already available to a limited number of women in specialist private clinics, and could well pave the way to a viable alternative for women to the old-fashioned male–female parental relationship . . .

Though she sees him in a coffin, Jane McLoughlin does not link this account of the redundant male to a vision of euthanasia; but we may dig out one of her pages and we can assume that it is connected with the means by which men will get turned into handbags – or lampshades. Near the beginning of her book, she writes:

> There is a real danger that society will begin to see the unproductive as burdens. Genetic engineering and abortion already make it possible to limit the number of babies born handicapped, and this could be taken much further. We could well find that the screening of television programmes on the ethical questions of euthanasia will start the process of softening society up before attempts to introduce suicide on demand, and that such attempts will gain wide support – within stringent legal guidelines, of course.
>
> This is treacherous ground, made all the more so by the political implications in the issues. This applies both to death on demand, and to abortion, because women who will have the numerical influence and the economic clout in the 1990s will use these issues as a significant political power base.

A spoor of argument can be followed here which leads to the edge of the alligator tank: men, being economically redundant, will be seen as burdens; women might use their power – within stringent legal guidelines, of course – to encourage the chaps to take the sensible exit.

We should all be enormously reassured to know that they will be acting legally. That *will* be a comfort.

188

The sisterly vision of male extinction – whether through the elimination of the sub-species or through the eradication of sexual differences – has, so far, failed comically and hopelessly to make any difference to the material world. The sisters who advanced that vision now look like hysterical twerps. We can say now, after twenty years, that it was always a profoundly anti-nature dream, inspired by terror of Eros and driven by Thanatos, resulting in a romance with death-delivering instruments of technological inhumanity. Its single greatest and most ludicrous failing was that the vision never allowed for the existence of desires which brought men and women together in sexual love and confirmed their union in new life. This is quite a big black hole in the cosmology of that Brave New World.

On the evidence of our own eyes and the basis of our own personal experience we can now say (well, I can) that there is, in the world of Nature and in the lives of humans, something ineradicable which no pseudo-fascist fantasy of high-tech superwomanry can or will dissolve or destroy. This something can be simply expressed. At the time of writing, a wry and intelligent rap record is making the beat in the clubs and discos of the young. Its title and main line is 'People are *still* having sex'.

The record is not more than incidentally addressed to those sisters, now far from their dance-floor years, who held that a sexual union with a man was a form of class betrayal: it is addressed more to the peculiar fact that, despite government health warnings on the practice and the discouragements of a consolidated establishment, boys and girls 'are *still* having sex'. An erect penis remains the indispensable personal tool of that apolitical pursuit and baby boys result from it in roughly the same number as baby girls. The young women who become pregnant have not, even after twenty years, absorbed the idea that conception should occur

– if it must – in bodies other than their own; or that their personal emancipation depends upon the culture and growth of foetuses in test-tubes. To the universal extent that young men and women have continued to pursue their desires for sex and love in firm relationships with each other, feminism has failed. Absolutely.

It has also failed, thoroughly and fatally, to ease or even to address the particular needs and difficulties of those young people (and many not so young) who are still having sex. Take a look around you. Walk the streets of the Granby triangle in Liverpool 8 or York Street in Hartlepool on a Saturday night. Cruise the bars of Dallas or Miami, the French Quarter of New Orleans or the beach-front in Venice, California. See the unemployed and unemployable girls, tottering round the streets in their micro skirts, bare legs, back-combed hair, plaster make-up and four-inch high heels, looking for romantic love or for a quick bunk-up which will give them a baby and a bit more money from the welfare services and the chance of a council flat.

Nothing in the existence of those girls and their boys has been improved by twenty years of feminism. They can expect to receive from the sisterhood no support, no help, no constancy. Feminism has failed so abjectly to improve the circumstances and alter the minds of those girls that it has to be questioned whether they can be included as members of the sorority. The sisterhood always said that it was interested in the conditions of all women, which it shared. That's not how it looks on York Street, Hartlepool, or the French Quarter of New Orleans.

A simple measure of this negligence and the failure of sororal care may be taken from the figures for teenage pregnancies. Adolescents are having sex in greater numbers than we did when we were young and more of them are becoming pregnant as a result. According to figures compiled

190

by the Brook Advisory Centres, the incidence of teenage conceptions rose from 58.7 per 1000 fifteen- to nineteen-year-olds in 1980 to 66.6 in 1988. In the same period, pregnancies among under sixteen-year-olds rose from 7.2 per 1000 to 9.4. In recent years the services of advisory clinics such as the Brook Centres have been cut for want of funds without, so far as I remember, a squak (that's a misprint but I think I'll leave it) of protest from those sisters now making their way through gilded salons who are more concerned with what they might wear to the Booker Prize dinner or the name of a reliable nanny or of a country-house hotel for a weekend of room-serviced bonking. If they cared a crumb for others than their selves, they would ensure, as a bare essential of sororal sympathy, that school-age girls and unemployed adolescents knew better than to become pregnant. A pregnancy in early or mid teens is such a complete catastrophe in the life of the girl (and, maybe, the boy) and so simply averted that the sisterhood should have been *clamouring* for better sex education and more efficient distribution of contraceptives for the young. We should be faced with their militant demands every time we open a newspaper or switch on a television. Instead of which, what? Silence.

My own opinion is that condom coin-machines should be placed in every school and that young girls contemplating intercourse should know for certain that they may receive a prescription for contraceptive pills, without argument, from a counsellor in the school. Let's not argue about whether or not they are going to fuck. We *know* that they are going to fuck. Let's make sure, as a first step, that they don't get pregnant. Then we can talk, if they want to talk.

Away from the salons and the bubble-baths in which the media sisters are now luxuriating, a social and fiscal catastrophe is rushing at us in the circumstances of poor

191

young women and their children. Income support and other forms of subsidy from public funds now amount to the annual payment of billions of pounds (variously calculated at between £1–5.5 billions) for single mothers and their children. In some municipal boroughs, fatherless children now outnumber those who know both their parents. The mothers may not work, for there are no jobs and they have no skills. The fathers will not give them support, for they have no money and are conferred neither rights nor dignities of paternity.

For those millions of unfortunates and their benighted children, the magazine covers of the sisterhood which squak about 'having it all' – jobs, money, possessions, children, love, sex, fulfilment – must seem nauseatingly rich. It dignifies this discrepancy between posture and reality, between the comforts of the sisters and the discomforts of the poor, to call it a failure of feminism: it is more properly named a genuine disgrace of our age.

If they have had any effect, the drives and demands of the sisterhood can be said to have extensively complicated and mutilated the lives of all young parents, rich or poor. The axioms of modern feminism have succeeded in exacerbating the difficulties of all parents in squaring their personal and sexual desires with the demands of life as an adult citizen in capitalist societies. You might see these complicating effects as failures or successes of sisterhood, according to taste and allegiance. I regard them as having being an unqualified disaster, not just for men.

An influential line in the feminist orthodoxy has always held fathers to be thoroughly redundant, inessential in economic contribution, deformed in emotional composition, more trouble than they are worth. Meanwhile the ideal of the mother – as embodiment of perfect love, as completed womankind – has been strong in the minds of some sisters;

though others offered discouragements. Shulamith Firestone was the first writer I came across who described the act of parturition as being 'like shitting a melon'; and that enticing account of a woman's oneness with her body and with nature has had a powerful pull on some of the sisters.

I last glimpsed a version of it when Ruby Wax was on my television, screaming at a theatre audience, telling pregnant women not to believe that they were about to experience a transport to heaven in the delivery-room. 'It's bloody fucking hell,' she roared. The audience was delighted.

In one of its aspects, the sisterhood can be seen as having driven towards the neutering of womanhood. The denigration of the pregnant woman and of maternity has been at least as powerful on one of its sides as the celebration of a woman's womanhood in pregnancy which has emerged from another side. There is, however, a distinct side of the sisterhood which seems to loathe the female in nature, being as fearful of Aphrodite as of Eros, and it expresses itself signally and unmistakably when it speaks about menstruation.

Despite the dominance of women's voices in the social and political argy-bargy of the West in the last twenty years, our culture and our times are exceptional in human organisations for offering no particular regard or dispensation to the menstruating woman. Since the introduction of mass-produced sanitary towels and, especially, since the pan-continental adoption of the internal tampon, women have been encouraged to act as if menstruation does not happen or, when it happens, makes no difference to them. That is the essential message of all that tampon advertising which enthuses about the products' gift to woman of the 'freedom' to get on with the rest of her life without interruption or embarrassment.

193

On the whole, the sisterhood has followed modern capitalism in its attitude to menstruation (setting aside those who believe that 'war is menstrual envy', who clearly have a different point of view). I think the foundation for the sisterhood's attitudes was given by Simone De Beauvoir in *The Second Sex*. 'This untidy event', she called it, words which were taken up by Susan Brownmiller who said that menstruation is 'a nasty inconvenience'.

According to this point of view, menstruation has been seen as a bodily intrusion disturbing cerebral or imaginative identities, one which, in its insistent demands of physiological reality, interferes with the fictional and fantastic, unreal lives which women feel that they are required to live or may prefer. As De Beauvoir put it: 'It is not easy to play the idol, the fairy, the faraway princess, when one feels a bloody cloth between one's legs; and, more generally, when one is conscious of the primitive misery of being a body.'

This 'primitive misery' may be set against another slogan of sisterhood which declares 'Our Bodies' to be 'Ourselves'; and we may be forgiven for being thoroughly confused by the disjunction. Are they glad or are they unhappy to find themselves a body (in what other form can a human being find itself?). The confusion originates, however, in the minds of the sisters who didn't know what to think for the best about their own essential gender and its primal imperatives. If they were confused about menstruation, they were hopelessly fucked up about motherhood.

On the issues of conception, parturition and maternity, the essential drives of the sisterhood have been, at least, twofold. Seeing, first, the family as a theatre of class antagonism, in which men impose the orders of bourgeois repression, some sisterly authorities have uniformly demeaned women who wished to be mothers of children. If the act of sexual intercourse was to be seen as 'sleeping with the enemy', then the admission of live sperm to a fertile womb, the bearing to term of a foetus and the giving of birth were seen as forms of absolute subjection, a delivery of self into slavery.

In that seams of sisterhood, enthusiasm grew for a complete withdrawal and abstention from intercourse with men, accompanied by an equally enthusiastic recommendation of alternative avenues of sexual gratification. Sheila Rowbotham records an issue of *Shrew* in the early Seventies, where a group of women argued for 'the alternative of homosexuality as a form of birth control . . . we could learn more about loving our own bodies and may even undo some of the damage society has done our sexuality and relate sexually with much greater awareness'.

(I haven't got a lot to say about homosexuality in this book because I am concerned with relations between men and women and with the family; but I want to add the observation in passing that the alliance between the sisterhood and the gay movement was, always, a kind of Brest-Litovsk arrangement. It was secured, apparently, because men who offered their penises to each other were safe for women who themselves distrusted penetration and its consequences.)

For sisters whose flesh was so weak that they could not resist the imperialistic prods of the phallus rampant, technological aid was urged and recommended. The evacuation of the enemy within was encouraged. Abortion was urged on any woman who had fallen foul.

We cannot know and will never know how many of the five or six million (Did Six Million Die?) foetuses aborted in the last twenty years had their lives stilled because their mothers saw the act of abortion as a commitment of sisterly solidarity. I *do* know, for sure, of a few such abortions in my own circle of acquaintance, only slightly fewer than the number of abortions of which I have personal knowledge where conception was felt to be an untoward nuisance in the domestic or professional arrangements of the woman (and/ or her man) and the foetus was evacuated as a form of contraception to suit cosmetic social needs. Of all the women – let me guess 200 – I have known to have had an abortion in the last twenty years not one was suffering from a medical condition, physical or psychological, in which her own health and/or the health of the baby might have been ruined by carriage to term.

If a Seventies sister eschewed abortion as a first remedy she was encouraged by the hoods to take advantage of new techniques of foetal scanning, allowing her to know whether she had conceived a male child and giving her the chance to eliminate the hated presence. If she gave birth to a boy, she was encouraged to reject him. 'For some women', writes Sheila Rowbotham, 'the contradictory experience of mothering boys has been the source of such pain that they have rejected sons.' In a wee while, when they are in full manhood, those little boys may have a few words to say to those mothers about their own pains.

The strictures of absolute denial were too much for many hundreds of thousands of young women who viewed themselves as being, otherwise, fully enlisted sisters. Among those young women who desired motherhood for themselves and could not count themselves class traitors in the desire, an accommodation was effected whereby the ideological apothegms did not necessarily have to be a spermicidal barrier to conception. For those young women, it was allowed that birth might be given, even to a boy, so long as men were excluded from the exercise of any power over the proceeding issue: the rights of men as fathers might not be admitted because, if they were, the mother must necessarily abandon herself altogether to the hated system of patriarchy.

The comprehensive exclusion of men was, from its earliest days, a signal characteristic of the methods, purposes and gatherings of the hoods. Spouses and lovers were not invited to attend those 'consciousness-raising' sessions in which cells of sisters pooled their experiences and shared their woes. Men were not invited to contribute to discussions in which women sought 'ways to attempt to change our own lives, so that we determine for ourselves the practical solution and the political solution for our own emancipation', the words with which Rochelle Wortis addressed the first British women's liberation conference in Oxford in 1970.

This exclusion was explained and defended by the sisters as a necessary act of self-defence. Men, they said, were so accustomed to having their way and to dominating the proceedings of meetings or the terms of conversation that women would submit to their powers if men were included. This line seems fabulously rich in sophistry twenty years later. What the sisters did not admit nor their fellow-travelling brothers contest was that an essential purpose of those discussions was to determine a working model of manhood and to determine the social and familial powers of men.

The brothers in the luggage compartment feared that the girls in the sealed carriages at the front were sniggering about their sexual performance and the potency of their parts; and they were right: that was happening. But something far more important was also happening. A bacillus was being brewed and conducted into the heart of our personal lives. By their definition of men as enemy, as mutant and as redundancy, the sisters were framing a social policy which limited or eliminated the rights of men as fathers. The definition of powers over children was an essential function of those sessions; and the exclusion of men from the discussion was more than a symbolic act: it declared, from the first, that rights of men were not to be admitted, save on the terms which the sisters determined.

It followed, automatically, from this determined exclusion and insistent control of parental rights that adherents of the sisterhood must not marry. To enter the state of matrimony was, necessarily, to accede to the laws and regulations of the bourgeois and patriarchal state and, consequently, to cede rights of paternity to men. Conception and parturition outside marriage conferred no rights of paternity upon the inseminating man, who was not recognised as having any existence in law.

According to the blurry compromises allowed within the sisterhood, a woman might allow penetration and conception, might give birth and have her child but she must, for the sake of her emancipatory potential, refuse to enter legal union with a man. The authorial sisters did not, as a rule, put the matter in exactly this light – for they saw, as I do not, that women were engaged in a fight for rights against a recalcitrant male establishment. Germaine Greer gave an exact expression of the general view of the sisterhood when she wrote in *The Female Eunuch*: 'If women are to effect a significant amelioration in their condition it seems obvious that they must refuse to marry. No worker can be required to sign on for life ... If independence is a necessary concomitant of freedom, women must not marry.'

In the non-marital, 'emancipatory' state of maternity which was allowable to sisters, men were perceived and designated as attendants, menials, supporters. The powers of the woman over the issue of fertility were supposed to be absolute; and the position of the father was held to be her gift, its measure subject to her own definition. Fathers should keep their place – designated as sponge-bearer and masseur in the delivery-room or, if they got dead lucky, as story-reader, pram-pusher and, of course, provider.

The poor saps who allied themselves with the sisterhood, as followers at foot sometimes dignified with the title 'partner' but more aptly named 'drone', found themselves in some fearful fangles as the sisters argued over their terms of definition. Scenes which were repeated in different guises many times in my own direct experience are recalled by Sheila Rowbotham who remembers 'bizarre spectacles at conference crèches, with one group of women demanding that men do the child care while others hiss the men who turn up for the crèche and insist their daughters go to a girls-only group'.

Those men had been given and had accepted a position never required of a married woman in the foregoing 100 years – the position of a domestic auxiliary, wholly without natural or legal rights, subject to contemptuous treatment or even to dismissal without notice at the whim of the sister he served. Many of those men believed, in their guilt over the notorious crime of patriarchy inflicted upon women of all ages, that they had to make up for their forebears in submission to their women. Saps. Assholes. Nitwits.

They delivered themselves into bondage, waiving rights of citizenship and paternity with carefree enthusiasm and unmitigated trust in the probity and good intentions of their sisters. How, they told themselves, should they not trust the moral soundness of women who said that they wanted to revolutionise the world as a whole and eliminate disadvantages deriving from gender?

Your heart must go out to them, poor fools. They believed that a revolutionary prospectus was in the making, that women represented the vanguard class whose determinations on policy should be followed by all willing subordinates. They believed the sisterhood would do them good. It was as an act of fraternal solidarity that they surrendered their rights as individuals into the hands of women who, unmistakably and directly, had declared men to be the enemy class in a war of gender hatred.

The sisterhood said that it was offering to break through repressive gender stereotypes, affording sexual and personal emancipation to all women and, they claimed, men. What they were actually doing in those meeting-rooms from which men were excluded and told to go and play with the kiddies' toys was forming and composing a definition of parenthood which would disenfranchise and disempower men as fathers. Those purposes and the 'definitions' of men which emerged have had immense consequences in the composition of our society and in the personal lives of our contemporaries.

Since 1970, the number of unmarried women giving birth has increased every year until now, when more than 25% of all live births are to unmarried women. An incalculable number of those women will subsequently have married the fathers of the children; but millions did not. Of those millions, a good number would not have had much choice, their men being unwilling to marry. Another good number chose to remain unmarried, with the agreement of the fathers. We cannot guess how many of the women who chose not to marry were directly influenced by the cardinal axioms of Germaine Greer and the other leading sisters. Quite obviously, many millions of those unmarried women came from poor and uneducated strata of society where books are not read and academic ideas, solipsistic or not, are not given instructional weight. It is simply impossible to reckon the influence of the sisterhood in the decisions of those poor girls who have had their babies without marrying the fathers; but it seems fair to imagine that a loud, fashionable and prominent establishment which declared, through all the megaphones of media communication, that it was more than all right for a girl to go it alone must have had some influence on the attitudes of those women.

From that mass of vagueness may be drawn a thread of certainty, supported by personal experience. I take it that my reader will, like me, know a certain number of women and men who decided not to marry when their children were born because they saw the way to the altar or the register office as the path to enslavement in bourgeois repression. They believed in free love and 'open' non-contractual relations. Some of them had flowers in their hair.

Nothing much in my adult life has been more painful than to witness or to hear about the devastations which have proceeded in the lives of some of my young men friends from that bold and buoyant renunciation of formal contract in their relationships with the women who bore the children they fathered. In return for their foolhardiness, many of the boys I grew up with have been worked over with a cruelty and inhumanity which would never be allowed between an owner and a dog. Some of them have had their lives comprehensively smashed as a result of that well-intended youthful abandon.

Among my friends at university, for example, were two brothers near in age, both revolutionary socialists, both clever and charming boys who were among the more enjoyable companions of that time. In their later twenties, they both fell in love and set up home with adherents of the sisterhood. The brothers openly and eagerly assented in the desires of those women to have children and they agreed not to marry. When their children were born, I believe that they were both loving and attentive fathers (I lost touch entirely with one of them; but I saw a lot of the other, younger, brother when his daughter was in her infancy and I can testify that no man has ever devoted himself more assiduously to his child).

The loves ended. I don't know the details. They don't matter. For whatever reason, the couples split up. The

201

mothers then lit out with the children, effectively abducting them. The brothers were powerless.

One of the sisterly mothers had a boyfriend in a European country. My former friend, her former lover and the father of her children, had a job in Britain which was simply un-transferable. He could not follow her and his children. I am told, by mutual and trustworthy friends, that he has spent all his spare time and most of his income in the last many years flying to see his children at weekends and paying for them to visit him in England. I hear that he has suffered massive pains in this history (a story which looks a lot more like 'her' story than 'his/tory'). I send him greetings and love across the decades along with the recommendation that he should put some of his remaining energy and political interest into ensuring that his own son should not suffer as he has.

The younger brother's woman lit out for Australia, taking their daughter with her. My friend's profession was trans-portable. If he wished to keep a connection with his own child, he had no choice but to follow to the other side of the world, to a society in which he knew nobody and a country towards which he had never, to my knowledge, shown the least enthusiasm. He went. As far as I know, he is still there. I hope he has found some happiness.

In these cases, the women's freedom to do and go where they chose involved an incontestable right to do whatever they liked with the children. They men were free to act, individually, as they chose, so long as their wishes and choices did not involve their children.

I know and can tell a baker's dozen of stories along the lines of those brothers'. On the few occasions when I have written in newspapers or spoken on radio about the abduc-tion of children by unmarried mothers or the denial of all rights of custody and care to unmarried, separated or divorced fathers, I have received letters from men (and, once, from the man's parents, the grandparents of the abducted child) to tell a similar story.

Though they bear a share of responsibility for their circumstances, having willed the state of the union or consented to it, those men have suffered an offence which ought to be criminal. It ought not to be allowable in law for any parent, married or not, to remove a child from another parent without consent. This is such an essential and obvious human right within an ordered society that it is astounding to find that it has been unasserted and unprotected, that unmarried men have been simply powerless to resist if the mother of their children takes a fancy to remove them. Those men have had, it goes without saying, no such power themselves. Any man who swipes his child and denies the mother rights of access, custody or care is likely to find his mug on the front pages of the gutter rags for his crime and the tug-of-love madness to which he has succumbed. It should be so: kidnapping children is a crime of such terrible power that it should be discouraged by all means; but that boot should be made to fit both feet of a parental union, marital or not, broken or intact.

Don't give me any crap about men caring less than women about their children or caring nothing for them. Don't try any of that boloney on me about men being less constitutionally capable of caring or 'nurturing' relations with their children. I really may run amok if I have to counter that monstrosity. It is nothing more than an aspect of the restrictive and sexist 'definition' of manhood which has been contrived by the hoods. It may not be applied to all men. I won't have it.

The elimination of the father has always been an essential purpose of the sisterhood. The assaults they have mounted upon marriage and the 'bourgeois' family may be seen as strategic ploys, clothed in ideological humbug and mumbo-jumbo, which were intended to vitiate men's rights of paternity and to transfer all parental rights to women. I sense, as I put these words down, that they sound like the expression of paranoid fantasy. Let me then give way again to Germaine Greer whom I find such an invaluable aide in the concise, if perverse, making of my point.

Writing about abortion in the *Independent Magazine* on 25 May 1991, Dr Greer summarised in three long sentences the case against the sisterhood which I have been trying to advance throughout this chapter. She said:

> Most societies have arranged matters so that a family surrounds and protects mother and child; our families having withered away so that only a male 'partner' remains, we find ourselves in a situation where the mother and child(ren) need often to be protected from him rather than by him. Our consensual liaisons grow less durable every year and, if the evidence of wife-battery, rape within marriage and child sexual abuse is to be credited, it is to be hoped that they will soon wither away altogether. The state having taken over the duties of children towards their parents (and allowed the childless among us to face the future without dread) it had better finish the job and take over the duties of the father towards the child.

Each of these sentences is infected with a perverted post hoc rationalisation which may hardly be untwisted. Germaine Greer has always, instinctively, repatriated and reconverted social phenomena to aggressive and destructive effects and here we see her compositional methods at their most sinuous and insinuating.

It is true that our families are withering away so that only a male 'partner' remains with mother and child/ren. She does not say so but Germaine Greer seems to imply that this withering away is a matter of pure historical accident or the workings of social dynamics. To a certain extent, the withering of the traditional, extended family close in ties of kin and rooted in near neighborhood has, indeed, resulted from impersonal forces. Chief of these has been the massive movements of migration within nation states and across continents, from the fields to the cities, from Europe to America, from the East Coast to the West, which have been the outstanding feature of social disintegration and recomposition in the last two hundred years. The withering of the traditional, extended family has also followed, evidently, from adaptations and reconformations, at microchip speed, in market economies and the responses of corporations which require individuals to move their homes from place to place in rapid order (a British Telecom manager once told me that BT expects its executives to 'relocate' about once in every five years).

On top of these impersonal forces of historical and economic movement, the family has also been subjected to a sustained and withering assault from a fashionable and influential establishment, partly instigated and led by Dr Greer. According to the sententious maxims of that establishment, many of them coined by Dr Greer, the family has been described as the prime theatre of sex war, in which the woman who conceives and bears her baby to term is a class traitor, in which the woman who marries the father of her child and thus confers some legal rights of paternity upon him has been regarded as making an alliance of servitude with the oppressor.

Does anybody doubt that some of the decomposition of the family in our age may be attributed to the influence of those maxims? Can we not, every one of us, testify to critical moments of decision in our personal and sexual lives in the

205

last twenty years when the outcome was influenced by the cardinal axioms of the sisterhood? Can we not, each one of us, name friends in dozens who have struggled in agonies of uncertainty about their 'political correctness' to know what to do for the best about their restless desires for stable love and sex in some form of 'consensual liaison', for children and for family? Do we not all know young men and women who entered marriage in tears of penitence and contrition, taking the car to the church or the register office with despair in their hearts at having contrived an act of class or sororal betrayal? Is anybody going to say that the imperative commands and ideological dispositions of the sisterhood have helped to make family life easier in our 'consensual liaisons'?

Those liaisons having, most definitely, grown 'less durable', as Greer avers, she hopes 'that they will soon wither away altogether'.

The justification she gives for this hope is 'if the evidence of wife-battery, rape within marriage and child sexual abuse is to be credited'. Here is another of her 'ifs' (like 'if women are the true proletariat') which are infinitely worthy of iffing. We may agree that, *if* that evidence is to be credited, marriage should be outlawed for the protection of women and their infants. But what if the evidence is not to be credited? What if it is fictitious? What if it has been falsified, grotesquely magnified and wilfully misrepresented? Then we may wonder about the motives of any writer who does not question that evidence but who seems to wish it to be credited. Germaine Greer appears to want to make the biggest and sorest possible trouble for men and women in families and, it must be said, she has succeeded mightily. Nobody in our time may have done more harm to families, most especially to fathers.

The dream of parricide is given voice in the last of her sentences. 'The state', she says, 'had better take over the duties of the father towards the child.' (Dr Greers does not, apparently, imagine that fathers might have something to say for themselves about this ambition.)

Here is the dream of the final solution for 'the Man problem' which has poisoned the collective sub-conscious of the hoods for a quarter of a century. In following this dream, the sisterhood has wrought its most singular effects, causing social consequences which it has claimed as marks of triumph and which I see as being top of the list of its most calamitous failures.

The state *has* become father to millions of the children of unmarried or unsupported mothers. Being thoroughly unfitted for the task, the state is making a God-awful pig's ear of the role, with consequences in the social and political life of the nation which are so disturbing that they may be considered with equanimity only by those who may be soon to depart this earth and won't be around to witness the miseries and devastations which are in store.

A generation has already come of age in the West which has no comprehension in its own direct experience of stable domestic and familial life. From Berlin to San Diego and from Oslo to Melbourne, tens of millions of children have been brought up, either by domestic auxiliaries or by arms of the state, in the absence of their natural parents, the mothers being at work and the fathers having taken a powder or having been shut out at the door.

Those kids are thoroughly and cluelessly confused about the ways of family and marital life. The instructional model which they have received in adult sexual and familial relations is, essentially, adolescent. Those kids have seen their parents behaving like the B-list cast from Dallas, hopping from bed to bed, from affair to affair, from marriage to marriage as if their teens and twenties never ended ('Nineteen Forever', in the words of another good pop song).

Germaine Greer once wrote a pithy piece about the transmutation by Western men of their promiscuous leanings into 'serial monogamy'. Through characteristic exclusion and bias, she did not see that the self-same habit has become universal to the women of her age. We all know women of thirty-five, forty-five, fifty-five who have been married and divorced two or three times or more and who are *still* looking for love and marriage with precisely the same set of yearnings which they brought to their first adolescent affairs (take a look at the blandishments in the Lonely Hearts' section of *Time Out*'s classified advertisements).

We all know middle-aged men and women (we may count ourselves among them) who – reeling from the shocks and traumas of their youth – will say 'I'm still waiting to find out what I'll do when I grow up'. The trials and difficulties of those individuals now in their middle years are genuinely affecting and demand sympathy; but they are trivial compared with the trials of their children, who have had to endure the withering of their parents' 'consensual liaisons' throughout their own infancies and adolescences.

The most fantastically unwarranted and indefensible claim of the sisterhood is that it has done those kids some kind of favour by depriving them of stable, loving, attentive and devoted parenthood from mothers and fathers. Swanking about their jobs, their salaries, their possessions, their clothes, their entertainments, their travels, their affairs, my generation is so smug and conceited in its satisfaction with itself that it cannot conceive of the idea that it might have inflicted unnecessary suffering on its children. We like to think and to say that we have introduced our children to a broader world of experience. We expect them to be grateful. I rather hope they will smack our silly old heads when we are lolling defenceless in our wheelchairs.

Few supporters of modern feminism would claim,

however, that an outstanding triumph of the movement has been to improve the lives of children in our age: they would say, on the contrary, that our deficiencies in child care result from the indifference of a male-oriented establishment which has refused to extend wider state benefits, such as nursery schools and day-care centres for working mothers. This complaint and demand may be seen as another aspect of the state-as-father dream and, of course, it is not addressed primarily to the benefit of the children but of the sister.

If you asked for the triumphs of modern feminism to be listed, you would probably be told that it has afforded women an unprecedented degree of economic freedom and that it has shifted the consciousness of society, allowing the personal to be considered at the heart of the political process, by citizens if not (yet) by leaders. Those are the answers I get when I ask; and I imagine that they are the answers you will receive if you ask.

If you agree that I have fairly described them, I want to discuss those victorious claims. You may not be surprised to learn that I regard them as being essentially untrue; or, to the degree that they are true, I regard them as signifying the failures rather than the successes of feminism.

First, let me talk about the economic freedoms supposedly achieved by the sisterhood through the militant extension of their demands.

The last time I was on the receiving end of this line of cant was when a middle-aged woman with a well-paid job on a London newspaper was taking me to task in a pub about an article I had written in a national magazine. She could not get it out of her head that I wanted to see women returned to the domestic servility which her mother had endured. Her mother had been, she said, 'chief household pet' to her father, wholly dependent upon his income. Her mother had been a slave, without the dignity of hire or wage. If feminism had done nothing else, this woman said, it had allowed women like her to achieve a degree of economic independence never allowed to her mother.

You can't argue – why should you want to? – with some of this. It is true that very few women had money of their own to spend before the mid-Sixties. It is true that very many women – most, perhaps, of the sisterhood of middle-class baby-boomers – now have money to spend which they have earned themselves. They are not dependent upon their men as their mothers were; and that must be nice for them (and nice, too, for the men who don't have to halve their pay).

No argument. No contest.

The point at which I disagreed with my critic and the point at which I take issue with the constant preenings of *Cosmopolitan, Ms* and all the other New Woman glossies is the point at which they describe this altered economic state as a form of financial 'independence'. That, it is not.

The term 'financial independence' has had a common and universal meaning in Western societies for more than 200 years, since the emergence of a capital-owning middle class. A man or woman would be described as being 'financially independent' if he or she had 'means'. 'Means' means capital. 'Independence' means having enough capital to live upon its proceeds, from interest or rents or the labour of others, without having to exchange your own labour with and from those who have capital. 'Means' means having income *without yourself having to work.*

People who have no means except their labour are dependent upon the income they can get from employers – those who have or control capital. Such a person, meaning most of us, cannot be called financially independent. The opposite is true. They are financially *dependent*. They depend upon their wages. They depend upon their jobs.

You must forgive me for this child's guide to the economics

of labour but it is, evidently, called for. My assailant in that London pub had obviously not grasped the concept. Neither has the sisterhood as a whole, for all its Marxian trimmings and deckings. They see the acquisition of jobs and salaries as 'deserved victories in equality', an expression used by Carol Sarler in a recent article in the *Sunday Times*. Even the old Lefties among them, who really should know better, reckon that a woman in employment has achieved a personal triumph of emancipation against the denials of a male-oriented capitalist class.

This point of view is so astoundingly inept in its political understanding that it fair takes your breath away. Remember that it comes from a group of people who, priding themselves upon their powers of political analysis, felt capable of teaching the world a few 'consciousness-raising' lessons.

What makes them think that women were given or took any degree of choice in their emergence, in great numbers, into the workforce?

Let me put this point another way.

If the emergence of women into the labour force and the acquisition of jobs and salaries is such a radical change, achieved against the will of an oppressive male establishment, and if it signifies the triumph of militant emancipatory demands, why does John Major like it so much?

I write this question on Tuesday, 29 October 1991. Yesterday, the Conservative Prime Minister of the United Kingdom launched an initiative requiring ministers of state and major corporations to take positive action, ensuring that women's names should appear on all lists of candidates for executive and managerial jobs. Observing the conventions of cant and nodding amiably in the direction of political correctness, Mr Major said that men in authority, controlling appointments, might not like the emergence of

211

women into positions of commercial power but they were going to have to get used to it. Everybody in his audience enjoyed a quick smirk of superiority. On this point of this jape, it is well-nigh impossible to find *anybody* who doesn't feel superior. Even the roly-poly Rotarians trenchering and troughing at their monthly luncheons in the market-town near my village congratulate themselves and each other that, in their bank, in their building firm, in their small factory, in their legal firm, any woman can take any job for which she is fitted by ability and application. If there genuinely exists a profit-minded group of male employers and executives whose members are averse to the hiring and promotion of women, I should genuinely like to meet them: they are such rare and antique specimens that they ought to be preserved as a national treasure.

Old duffers' clubs such as the Churches of England and Rome, the Marylebone Cricket Club or the Garrick Club *are* still snorting and puffing about the admission of women on equal terms; but most of these are such marginal institutions of British life that they can, with ease and equanimity, be left to sort out their sclerotic pains for themselves. I exclude the Church of England from this benign allowance. The CoE's continuing inadmission of women to full powers and rites of priesthood is an indefensible barbarity in my book, enormously damaging to the institution itself, and I have personally opposed its specious reasonings both in my journalistic work and in the Parochial Church Council of my village.

(I know what you're thinking. 'What about Parliament?' you are screaming. 'Is that a marginal old duffers' club?' I hear you. I'm coming to Parliament. Just give me a minute.)

If you really want to know how women are viewed in the mainstream of Western life, go and talk to the personnel director of a major international corporation such as Nissan or Ford or IBM. This is such a valuable and instructive experience that I sincerely urge it upon anybody who may get the opportunity. What you will discover is that there is no division between the giants of international capitalism and the pseudo-Marxians of the sisterhood, with Mr Major smiling and nodding and ushering between them.

At the vast Nissan plant at Washington, near Sunderland, I asked why there were so few women to be seen on the factory floors and relatively few in the offices. The passionate sincerity of the Nissan executive who replied could not be doubted. 'We are desperate to employ more women,' he declared. 'We do everything we can to encourage them; but the trouble is that very few women apply for jobs here. In this area, car making is seen as being a man's job.' At a nearby factory making vacuum cleaners, he said, the imbalance in applications and jobs is reversed. Hardly any men work there, he said, because vacuum cleaners are seen as being work for women's hands. Executives at both companies are tearing their hair out trying to see how to get round the blockages of those prejudices *in their potential workforce*.

In the course of quite a long run through and among Western corporations and businesses, I have only once come across a major company in whose employment practices an obvious and incontestable discrimination against women was evinced at the most senior levels of management. That corporation was Occidental Petroleum of Los Angeles, California, while it was under the direction of Dr Armand Hammer. When I was intimate with this corporation, in the Eighties, 'Oxy', as it is known, had only one woman director on its main board and none (as far as I can remember) at vice-president or president level.

But Armand Hammer was in his eighties during the 1980s and he was still nodding at the helm into his nineties and the 1990s. He was an old dinosaur who believed that women were

213

good for nothing more than taking notes, making coffee and bending their bottoms over his desk. His sexual attitudes and employment practices were a genuine relic and I expect that, now he has gone, they have gone with him.

Elsewhere, in the world of hard dollars and cruel commercial necessities, servants of corporations cannot afford to exclude women from appointments at all levels. They have got to get them, to include them and to keep them and they know it.

This requirement has got bugger all to do with feminism. The personnel director of IBM would not, I guess, give two spits for any -ism which didn't begin with capital, especially not a wasm. Ditto John Major; ditto my local Rotarians. Sentiments or the claims of natural justice do not enter the frame of their calculations. Their bottom line is that they cannot satisfy their labour needs nor supply the technologies of their production without being able to tap the entire adult workforce.

If you view this commercial development with enthusiasm, seeing it as a means to emancipation, we may well part company. I find little cause for pleasure, relish or satisfaction in the prospect; but, then, I've got a strange view of work: I tend to think that people ought to do a great deal less of it.

I tend to think that it's something short of the perfect sanctification of the divine gift of life to spend 90,000 adult hours in the service of capital and profit and most of the remaining hours asleep.

I tend to think that young men and women might get more pleasure out of their lives, to which they ought to be entitled, if they had time to enjoy each other's loves and the incomparable, irreplaceable delights of their children's infancies. I tend to think that 'workaholism' is a curse worse than crack and more destructive to our social well-being.

I tend to think that the subjection of men and women to the slavery of worthless work for the promotion of consumer markets is an abomination of our age; and I tend to think that the fact that women now have to put up with that subjection in the same measure as men – while also being largely responsible for domestic and family life – may be numbered among the most distressful aspects of our days. To think, as others tend to do, that we have counted this development as 'a deserved victory in equality', as a triumph of emancipation, is so tragic that it could make you weep, if you were me.

But I must tend to be weird, I guess.

Even if you don't see work my way, you must admit that it is one of the more piquant paradoxes of modern history that the wearing of a business suit and the carrying of an executive briefcase should now be seen, as they are, as marks of female emancipation. It's as if the western world went for a loop over forty years, back to the days of the Edsel, the Zephyr-Zodiac and the dream-house in the suburbs. Forty years ago, the man in the Grey Flannel Suit, wearily resting his head on the commuter train from White Plains, was the very image of alienation and crushed individuality against which much of the spirit of the young in the post-war generations was directed. If there was one thing we could say for sure it was that we were not going to replicate and endure his miseries. Now we find that personage, doubled by gender, celebrated as a hero of personal emancipation – if it happens to be dressed in a grey skirt rather than trousers and a tie. If it has gonads, it is, of course, a figure of repression, of near-naked phallic aggression and ambition.

The Woman in the Grey Flannel Suit was born because the technologies of contraception and abortion allowed industry, for the first time, to recruit workers from the whole adult population. Since they take their origin in capitalism, her difficulties, frustrations and exhaustions may not be blamed, primarily, on feminism. But feminism has certainly exacerbated those difficulties, especially through the continuing insistence of the sisters that men and women have divergent and antagonistic interests at work and in the home. The language of sex war has been shifted along the trenches from the command-posts of the kitchen to the corporate boardroom, with awful results in both places.

By exquisite paradox, that language, originally cloaked in a fiery aura of Marxian subversion, incidentally serves the interests of capitalism, as those interests are presently felt and expressed. It urges women, with militant fire in their bosoms, to pursue the holy grail of career and advancement, struggling with the dark forces of the male-oriented world of business and the professions. It exhorts women, as good sisters, to make an accommodation and resolution of their maternal interests with their demand for financial 'independence' and, in both spheres, to regard their interests as being distinct from and inimical to the interests of men. It places upon them a burden of responsibility and guilt which is simply unmanageable and unbearable.

I realise that this is a mouthful. I am trying to express in general terms the prevailing attitude, espoused by feminists, towards the position of working mothers. I am trying to say that this general position has been described in terms of sex war in which, it is said, the difficulties of women can only be resolved by their militant claiming of rights from an ungiving society. Let me find another voice of authority to state this position.

The clearest and most concise expression I know of the orthodox view is the one expressed by Benjamin Spock in the *revised* version of *Baby & Child Care*, the one where he had thought again about his original strictures about the natural place of woman at home and wanted to enter some liber-

216

tarian modifications. This is what he said when he had thought again:

> When I said I thought fathers and mothers had an equal responsibility in child care I didn't mean that they must necessarily put in exactly the same number of hours at it . . . I meant . . . that they have an equal *right* to a career with the least possible interruption.

Here we have the great uncle of the West, the instructional authority who gave America its bible on the raising of children, expressing the view that the raising of children, which he might treat as being the supreme care and joy of an adult life, is a kind of interruption in the individual adult's *right* to a career. Spock wrote those words because he had been knocked around by the feminist establishment for saying, in earlier editions, that women ought to be full-time mothers at home. The revisionism he has committed here is a horrible and degrading act of submission to a hectoring gang of fanatics and it reminds me of seeing a Professor of Physics in a dunce's cap on the steps of the Great Hall of the People, confessing his political incorrectness.

You are thinking, aren't you, that I want to see women returned to full-time housewifery and motherhood? I do not. I am merely trying, for the moment, to explore some of the consequences and failures of feminism.

I saw some of these consequences and failures most vividly at a working women's conference I was invited to attend last year. In one of the conference rooms, a small company was giving a seminar on the child-care arrangements it offered to working mothers.

The representatives of that company stressed the flexibility of its provisions. The company had, they said, given a great deal of thought to the real needs of working mothers

217

and they realised that they had to frame the hours of the service they offered to suit the real requirements of career women, rather than impose strictly set hours which made the working day's timetable of the mother more complicated. A mother might drop off her child at the company's nursery rooms as early as 7.00 a.m. If she needed to work late at the office, to go out for a drink with colleagues or a client, she could leave the child with them until as late as 8.00 p.m. The company was happy to take children as young as two years and they would look after those children, if need be, until they went to school.

This company would not exist unless it met a need. I believe the picture it gave of the demands of work upon the time of young parents is largely reliable (I am glad to say that, for once, the young women in the picture are not media trendies of the sisterhood: the women at that conference were mostly executives in the public sector, some in business and banking). Following the prospectus of that company, I think we can say with sound confidence that we have contrived a state in which both parents, mother and father, are now likely to say that they never see their infant children fully awake during the week and that, at the weekends, those parents are likely to be too exhausted by their working week and by the additional work they may have to carry home to take active and pleasurable interest in their children.

This state of being, adverse and cruel both for parents and for children, may be thought to be an unqualified misery which may only be relieved by radical political thought and structural engineering in which the interests of all members of the family are given central priority. That's how I see it. Feminists and the powerful establishment they have affec-ted see it differently. Fathers being excluded from their minds and from the distribution of rights and powers in the family, they tend to regard the woes of working parents as being unique to women and as being capable of solution through the provision of more child care conducted by others – in crèches, day-care centres and nursery schools, the State-as-Father again. The exclusion of the father, which has been a cardinal purpose of feminism since the beginning, has become a habit of orthodox political thinking.

This exclusion and the extent to which it has become an aspect of orthodoxy was vividly demonstrated in a television seminar on the position of working mothers shown on Channel 4 in the early autumn of 1990. This was a whole hour of television, conducted in an atmosphere of scrupulous solemnity, in which six experts, including a number of prominent spokeswomen from government and opposition, quizzed representatives of employers' groups and theoreticians on the family.

The whole of the first twenty-five minutes of the programme was devoted to the requirements of the modern economy and the needs of business for women workers. Nearly half of the programme was over, therefore, before the needs of parents and children were brought into the picture. I don't diminish the importance of economic imperatives but, as with the Spock quote, I just want to enter an incidental alas and alack that the brazen image of the great god Profit should be trundled like a juggernaut over the needs of individuals.

When the needs of parents were at last considered on this programme, parents meant, exclusively, mothers. Fathers were mentioned – the word 'father' was mentioned – only once in a whole hour; and that came in a way and in a context which I take to be acutely revealing.

An American academic, asked to sum up her general attitudes to the debate in Britain about women at work, said

219

that it was extraordinary to her that we were so far behind the rest of the developed world.

In America and elsewhere in Europe, she said, these questions had been settled twenty years ago. Nobody in America ever wondered any longer whether children's interests and emotional health might be damaged by having mothers go out to work. 'We take it for granted', she said, 'that they are not damaged by having fathers who go out to work.'

Both assertions are mistaken (besides being mildly offensive in their tone). My family and I lived in America for long stretches in the Eighties and I doubt if any question was more commonly, even tediously, discussed among the people we met than the effect on children of their being in the care of others, not their parents, from their earliest infancy. It may be that we did something to provoke this topic and that all our hosts and guests truly wanted to discuss was baseball and Star Wars; but I can assure you that it didn't look like that. And, more, the Americans I know – men and women – do not take it for granted that children are unaffected by the absence of fathers at work. The men certainly don't take it for granted that the children are unaffected. I have spent forty days and forty nights in the wilderness of trips around the world with middle-aged American businessmen who did nothing but moan about their absences from their children. In this sense, America may genuinely be a decade or so ahead of Britain; because there, at least, the rights and needs of men as fathers are given some place, formally and informally, in debates on the family.

In Britain, we are still accustomed to think that it is women's business alone to square the conflicting demands of work and child care. So long as we continue to think that way, we shall assuredly go on making modern life impossibly painful for women and bleakly unrewarding for both men and women. The general presumptions upon which that attitude rests have been determined by modern feminists in their hectic exclusion of men from the powers and rights of parenthood. The fearful mess of pains which are being borne by women today result, themselves, from the influence of those feminist determinations and they will not be eased until we find another style of address to our national dilemma, which is the question 'Who brings home the bacon? Who brings up the baby?' Feminism has failed, comprehensively, to provide whole, happy and politically radical answers to this question. As a body of attitudes, it is incapable of providing those answers for it declares, from its heart, that the interests of men and women are naturally antagonistic.

My own suggestions, based on the presumption that the interests of men and women are usually identical and where they differ are invariably symmetrical, follow in the next chapter. In that chapter, I shall be coming back to the position of women at work and taking a lump hammer to 'the glass ceiling' of obstruction for women in achieving senior positions. The existence of that glass ceiling must have been at the back of your mind. It is at the back of my mind, too.

First, we must talk about Parliament and a wider world of impersonal politics. Here is the arena in which the reader may feel that the claims of the sisterhood are found to be most obviously sound, where the resistance of a male-orientated establishment of authority has most clearly resisted the rights of women and the claims of feminism.

I don't think so. To my way of thinking, it is in this arena that feminism has failed most signally and done us all the greatest harm in its failure.

The tenth anniversary was celebrated in 1990 of the founding of The 300 Group, which campaigns for equal numbers of men and women MPs. More than seventy years have passed since Nancy Astor took her seat in the House of Commons, the first woman to be elected. More than sixty years have passed since the final extension of the franchise to all adult women. The push to provide men and women with equal rights of franchise and representation has unquestionably been the dominant movement for constitutional change in this century; and, as the century enters its last decade, now is a good moment to take stock; and to ask again, how long, O Lord?

By any reckoning, the movement in its modern personification must be counted a failure. The figures for women's representation in the House of Commons are as discreditable as they are dismaying. In the seventy years since Nancy Astor's election in 1919, only 141 women have taken seats in the House of Commons. The last twenty years of liberation for women have brought no more than glancing adjustments to the composition of the House of Commons. Following the General Election of 1970, twenty-six women were returned, approximately 4% of the total number of MPs. In 1974, after the second election of that year, there were twenty-seven women MPs. After the 1979 election which sent Margaret Thatcher to Downing Street, the number had *reduced* to nineteen women. In the autumn of 1990 when The 300 Group was ten years old, there were fifty-nine women MPs, 6.6% of the total. The General Election of 1992 returned 59 women to the House of Commons.

If this rate of growth were to be sustained, with the number of women MPs rising by 60% every twenty years, the target of The 300 Group would be achieved around the year 2069, exactly 150 years after the voters of Plymouth sent Nancy Astor to the House of Commons. The 'structural' changes proposed by the Labour Party, including the forced selection of women candidates, might accelerate the process. It is even possible that, by these measures, the number of women in the House might reach three figures by the second quarter of the next century. There's rejoicing for you, ladies.

The reasons why women do not go to the House cannot be explained simply by the obstructions of male prejudice, though we may guess that they exist in some pockets. Where those pockets may be, I cannot tell. On the last page of *The Female Eunuch*, Germaine Greer quotes from Long's *Eve*, published in 1875 and saying '. . . among the disbelievers of revealed religion I have not found during a life of half a century, a single opponent to the doctrine of equal rights for males and females'. I can supply a contemporary version of that observation: in a life of nearly half a century, I have not found among citizens who are interested in politics a single opponent to the doctrine of greater, if not equal, representation of women in Parliament.

Constituency selection committees of all parties have shown themselves willing to choose women candidates; and the electorate has shown itself willing to return women members. Despite the evidence to the contrary, let's assume that male prejudice is a genuine obstruction to women candidates; let's guess that male prejudice might account for the absence of fifty women MPs: that still leaves 200 women MPs who are missing from the House for some other reason or reasons.

What? Why?

The most obvious reason, agreed and endorsed by all observers, is that parliamentary life is inimical to family life. Routine business at the Palace of Westminster is scheduled on the careless presumption that members are not burdened with domestic responsibilities. Committees meet during the day; sittings of the House begin after lunch and continue through the evening; votes are often taken late at night; all-night sessions regularly occur towards the end of parliamentary terms.

Where an MP represents a constituency outside the

capital, he will also be expected to spend his weekends travelling to and from London and conducting surgeries, opening fêtes, standing for reselection and all the rest of the local hoop-la.

Thus the MP's job is like a miner's: it can hardly be done without full-time domestic support. Self-evidently, it is near impossible for a man to work all day at the coal-face, five or six days a week, and to be simultaneously responsible for child care, laundry, meals, house-cleaning, shopping and attendance at the PTA. If he is to do the job, the MP and the miner *must* have a wife.

We cannot know how many women *and men* who might have been MPs have been put off the idea of a political career by the certain fact that election to the House would infallibly and inevitably mark the effective end of their lives as active mothers. I have. We may be certain, however, that the absence of women as MPs will continue so long as the routine practices of the House of Commons presume that members are content to see their children only on Sunday afternoons and for two weeks in August. I have never heard anybody question this verity. I do not question it.

What, then, has the sisterhood done? What difference has it made? Here, in Parliament, we see a vastly powerful arm of the state wholly controlled by men and excluding women by reason of its antique internal business procedures. Outside the Palace of Westminster, in the country as a whole, we see a universal desire that more women should stand and be elected. Even within the House itself, we hear no voices of opposition to the admission of more women.

So why hasn't it happened? What's the hang-up? Why is Britain, uniquely in the north-west of the planet, still represented by a legislative assembly which reflects the social composition and distribution of powers of the nine-teenth century?

The sisters have failed to effect change. They have failed to make a difference. I suspect, in a corner of my mind, that they do not want change.

Why have there not been Private Members' Bills brought forward in every session of Parliament to advance proposals for revised hours of sitting and fewer post-prandial deliberations on policy? As far as I know, the last major attempt to effect such changes was made in 1967, when Richard Crossman was Leader of the House. That's twenty-five years ago – the same twenty-five years during which the claims of feminism have resistlessly advanced. In the whole of that quarter century, the sisterhood has never once contrived a public and parliamentary campaign, catching the desires of the electorate as a whole, to change the place. How many supporters of The 300 Group have you ever met? How many of them tried to enlist your support in a public campaign to secure the changes which everybody wants? How many times have you seen Clare Short MP or Harriet Harman MP on television shouting to the rooftops that the compositional antiquity of our respective assembly must be changed *right now*? How many times have they risen in the House of Commons itself to make that demand or threatened to chain themselves to the Mace until it is granted? To my knowledge, the principal concerns of women in the House have been expressed over the provision of cloakrooms, crèches and restaurant tables in the building for their better comfort.

Feminism has failed, absolutely, to get its act together over Parliament. The hoods have never agreed a unified line of policy or a collective and singular form of expression. They have not, in fact, known what they wanted or thought. To an immeasurable degree, powerful in my mind, their indecision and ineffectiveness has resulted from their thumping insistence that the personal is political. They have often said

225

that women's natural interests and preoccupations lay in personal relations and that the institutions of government, male supremacist all, were simply irrelevant to those interests. As far as I can see, The 300 Group is not mentioned anywhere in Sheila Rowbotham's history of British feminism. Throughout the whole of that broad survey, I cannot find a single page of discussion about the question of women's representation in Parliament. Perhaps I have missed something. Perhaps the hoods have.

What have they imagined would happen to the House of Commons? That it would simply fade away with a regretful sigh, acknowledging its irrelevance? That it would contritely abandon the business of debating Bills and passing Acts of law because that wearisome task of government had been rendered redundant by the political process of the personal?

It does look as if the sisters were thinking that way. It does look – to me at least – as if they have been content to let the House of Commons stay the way it is because it is a graphic and powerful symbol of male authority.

Part of the truth is that it suits the sisters not to have a reformed House of Commons because its continued anti-quated existence is a living proof of male supremacist attitudes. Anybody who doubts that ours is a patriarchal society will be directed to run his eye over the green leather benches and count the number of women. End of argument.

Not quite.

It is intolerable that men should continue to outnumber women in parliamentary seats by roughly fifteen to one. A modern society simply cannot be governed judiciously from such an absurdly imbalanced assembly. To think that our Parliament is likely to enter the twenty-first century with the composition of the nineteenth century is, admittedly, wildly comical; but it is also unacceptable. Change must be demanded and instituted now.

Since nobody else seems to have any idea how to correct this vertiginous imbalance in our national life, I may as well advance the Lyndon Plan. It sounds daft: but it is not so absurd as the fact that, in 1990, women made up 6% of the membership of the House of Commons.

My suggestion is that an MP's duties should be made the subject of a 'job-share'. Speaking informally, the job is already shared, given the MP's dependence on his wife. Generations of women MPs from Barbara Castle to Harriet Harman have been heard to complain that what they really need is a wife. So why don't we give them a parliamentary spouse (they would not be obliged to treat their union as being connubial)? A proposal along these lines was made in early 1992, in a Private Member's Bill proposed by Teresa Gorman and supported by Clare Short and Edwina Currie. I had the same idea in 1991 and expressed it in an article I wrote for the *Independent*. The article was not published because the idea was felt to be so wildly eccentric that it could not be admitted within the pages of a serious newspaper. A year later, the same idea was being debated in the House of Commons itself.

This is the idea: why not have two MPs, a man and a woman, dividing and sharing the work? They could take it turn and turn about to be at the House or in the constituency, to be sitting in committee or voting in the chamber. This reform would instantly give the House of Commons 50% female membership. It could also, if both MPs were paid the same amount as one is paid today, go a long way towards remedying the present laughable inadequacy of MPs' pay.

What would be that cost? I don't know. Say, sixty million pounds. Beans for the most important structural reform in our representation.

You will ask 'what would happen when they disagreed on

a vote?' Are you kidding? What do you think the Whips do? Sit on their whips? MPs aren't *allowed* to decide for themselves how to vote: dissent is not included in the job description. If they couldn't agree on the casting of their vote in committee, they would have to abstain. Easy, see.

What about Cabinet Ministers? What about the Prime Minister?

The answer seems to be that, when a constituency is represented by a member of the Government at Junior Minister level or above, it will have to return three MPs – two for the job-share and one for office (chorus here of 'Three, three the ri-i-i-vals').

Then they could conduct business at sensible hours, take shorter holidays, do more work, pass more Bills . . .

Pass more Bills? Let's stop there. Maybe this isn't such a good idea, after all. If you have a better idea, act on it. Don't wait for feminism to make the change. The sisters will go on sitting on their hands and on that obnoxious and infantile complacency which declares the personal to be political and which consequently treats the political as being irrelevant if it is not, directly, personal. See where that has got us – not absolutely but in a sense.

It got us Ronald Reagan and Richard Nixon; it got us Margaret Thatcher and Helmut Kohl; it got us continuing arms' races and Cold War; it got us a Falklands War; it got us the rampant, materialistic 'supply side' economics of political conservatism; it got us broken and enfeebled opposition parties in Europe and America; it got us no change in constitutional arrangements that had been out of date for half a century; it got us the continuation, long past its purposeful life, of two-party systems which failed thoroughly to represent the interests of thirds of the electorate in Britain and America; it got us a generation without political leadership; it got us Dan Quayle firmly in the running to be President of the United States in the last years of the century.

Now come on, you will be saying: this really is too much. There may have been rhetorical excesses and political uncertainties in modern feminism and its influence upon personal lives may not have been altogether benign; but anybody who is going to blame the Falklands War on Germaine Greer is stretching their case beyond the breaking point of sympathetic credulity.

All right, I give in; I admit it; I have gone too far. Germaine Greer is *not* responsible for the Falklands War, absolutely: just in a sense.

This is the sense. It is not so limited and partial as you may suppose.

One of the more enticing and intriguing historical questions of the last half of this century to ask is: what happened to the promise of the Sixties generation? What happened to their radical desires? Why did those energies, which seemed to offer the prospect of comprehensive change within the institutions and the customs of the West, result in so little discernible change?

We can agree, can't we, that there has been very little change? The greatest change in our era has been the collapse of state socialism in the East and the end of the Cold War. That sea change in the century was not caused, effected or influenced in the least by the desires or beliefs of the radical Sixties baby-boomers. They had nothing to do with it. There are raisin-brained people in Britain who appear genuinely to believe that the removal of Cruise missiles from British soil results directly from the efforts of the Greenham Common women. They are fooling themselves as much as the Young Communists of Salisbury who said the Berlin Wall had to be built to keep out Westerners. You will not meet a man less enthusiastic for the politics of the Reagan/Thatcher years than I. There is, however, no question in my mind that it was the arms expansion policies of the Reagan administrations, finally and critically the Star Wars initiative, which destroyed the Soviet Union and removed the threat of thermonuclear exchanges between the superpowers.

I know what I'm talking about. I visited Moscow in the Eighties more times than I can count. I was in a position to talk frequently to influential members of the Soviet leadership, even up to the Politburo level. I saw what was going on in their minds from 1985, when the Star Wars, initiative was declared, until the Moscow Summit of 1988 which, effectively, ended the Cold War. Those boys were *desperate*. They knew, with a chill in their vitals, that if America lifted the arms race into space, they were finished. They knew that their Third World industrial and military technologies were inadequate to the competition and that they could not finance modernisation, not least because nobody would sell them the kit and they couldn't afford to invent it. Between 1985–7, they threw every diplomatic and negotiating punch they could find in their locker to dissuade the Americans from pursuing SDI. They said that all the foregoing arms deals and negotiations, including the ABM Treaties and SALT, would be off, off, off. The Americans told them to take a walk. In the end, the Soviets meekly folded their hands. The stakes were impossible and they couldn't bluff another day.

Those men in Moscow and in Washington cared for the opinions of the Greenham Common women about as much as Margaret Thatcher cared what Ben Elton thought about her. If you could take a computer graph of their consciousness, you would find that the yawpings outside the perimeter fence at Greenham Common didn't even make a blip.

As in most other matters of major political importance in our adult lifetimes, the radical generation of the Sixties was irrelevant to the most important political shift in the entire century. Absolutely irrelevant.

I asked, first, if we could agree that little has changed. Do we agree? Look at all the most important functions of government and the operations of its leading and most powerful institutions. Look at our systems of representation and at the machinery of Parliament, Congress and Bundestag. Look at the character of ministries of state and the powers they dispense over taxation; defence; education; health; housing; transport; labour and industry. Can you say that there is, in any of these political institutions or their practices, an outstanding and radical difference in the Nineties compared with the early Sixties – a difference undeniably attributable to the political intelligence, radically applied, of the post-war generation?

I don't see it. In the early Eighties, I believed that the West German Greens were in a position to effect radical changes in the political dispositions of that country; but I think you would be hard pressed today to name many. Otherwise, the only profound difference I can see in the political arrangements of our present time compared with thirty years ago is in the increasing federalisation of powers between European nation states; and that change, manifestly, has had nothing whatsoever to do with the desires of the Sixties generation, most of whom, if they gave it any thought, opposed it.

Do we agree? Are we of the same mind?

If we agree, my original question becomes more pressing and disquieting. Why has that generation, my generation, caused and effected no radical change in the political systems of government in the West?

You would not have predicted this inert stability. Considering the passionate political engagements of that generation in its youth, you would (I did) have imagined that by now, when we are well-advanced into the years of our fullest maturity, comprehensive changes would have been completed. For a start, we could have expected that Britain would have been non-nuclear for at least fifteen years and that the military establishment of Britain's post-war, post-Imperial years would have been thoroughly dismantled and reorganised.

When I was twenty in 1966 and expecting that my generation would have come to the fulfilment of its political promise within a decade, it would not have been credible to me to imagine that, nearly twenty years later, Britain might launch and fight yet another of those bizarrely deluded post-Imperial excursions into the far (Malaya, Kenya, Cyprus, Belize) world which had studded my infancy and adolescence. I was certain that, by then, the population at large would be resting easy with the idea that, as a small trading nation off the continent of Europe, we were exceedingly well placed to provide for our needs without wasting money sending aircraft carriers and nuclear submarines to hoist the flag over shepherds' huts around the world.

The moment of deepest political despair for me came in 1982, when I was staying in Liverpool, a year after the riots of 1981 and the Ruritanian fantasies of that year's Royal Wedding. It was unbearable to be living in those surroundings and to be blasted with the injunction to rejoice at the recapture of South Georgia while gangs of hopelessly impoverished black kids put on stunts of joy-riding and battled with the police on the streets of the Granby triangle. If Britain was sending expeditionary forces to chastise tinpot dictators in the Southern hemisphere even while its ghettos burned at home, there was little choice but to acknowledge that my generation was politically worthless, *inutile*.

I would never have believed that, when I was middle-aged, teachers, doctors and nurses would be worth less in financial benefits and social prestige than they had been in 1960; and that the systems of education and health service would be in such decay that my own contemporaries should think they served their families best by paying for private education and medical treatment.

I would never have believed that, when we had come of age and should have been in power, working people of all ages and all classes would be required to work longer hours for less pay than the members of the generations we succeeded.

I would never have believed that there might be more teenage pregnancies and abortions in 1990 than 1970.

I would never have believed that, out of all the scintillating, captivating, ingenious, educated, generous and philanthropically minded young people of my age not one single individual would emerge into adulthood, neither in Europe nor in America, who would be the figurehead of inspired leadership. I supposed that we would throw up cynosures like Adlai Stevenson or Bobby Kennedy, leaders of whom we would say and feel 'That's it: that's the voice we need to hear; here is the person who genuinely represents our feelings and desires.' You may take this to be a Messianic fantasy; but I imagined that there would be scores of such magnetic leaders and public servants, Disraelis and Trotskys of our age, Voltaires and Thoreaus.

Where the hell are they? Look around. Can you name one individual in the West, aspiring to political office, who genuinely and comprehensively embodies and personifies the libertarian and radical desires of the Sixties generation which is now middle-aged? Al Gore? Dick Gephardt? Neil Kinnock? William Waldegrave? Jack Straw? Sue Slipman? Dan Quayle? What the hell happened to us?

The answers to these questions probably ought to be complicated; but I want to make a simple observation. I want to say that the disabling influence of the great feminist terror is among the answers. The radical young of the Sixties were split down the middle by the axioms of feminism and were politically disenfranchised and disempowered by them. If the personal was political, what point might there be in addressing the institutions which embodied and dispensed political power? If the enemy of the educated, white, liberal, middle-class woman was the educated, white, liberal, middle-class man with whom she might share her bed, what need was there for either of them to puzzle over the complications of political allegiance in the wider world? Might as well turn over and go back to sleep.

When my own sister, my own wife, my own daughter is determined to regard me as her enemy and as the agent of the political institutions which I might wish to change, how should I change them?

Had the electoral system of Britain been reformed in the Seventies – which might have been the first task of my generation if we had been politically coherent and effective – Margaret Thatcher would not have been Prime Minister. The Falklands fiasco would probably not, then, have taken the shape of a battle group of gung-ho boys sailing south to get their legs blown off and their faces boiled in napalm. To that indefinite extent, the sisterhood has a share of the blame for the Falklands War; and I sincerely hope that political thought may not give Dr Greer a dose of those intimately personal and queenly rejoicings she enjoys at the sight of men fighting.

SEVEN

No More Sex War

If you have travelled with me this far, it might have crossed your mind to feel that some militancy in men is called for. It may seem that, to borrow a phrase, the only corrective to the social injustice suffered by men and to the vile incubus distilled and distributed by the hoods would result from an aggressive assault by men, carrying the sex war back to the bunkers and map-rooms of sisterhood from which it originated.

Some men are, apparently, beginning to feel this way. Following the appearance of some articles of mine, I have had letters from a number of them. Those who have written are mainly young men in their late twenties and early thirties who are bitterly angry that their youths and college days were poisoned and spoiled by the activities and claims of the hoods. Some of them have invited me to join their groups or sign up with the campaigns and movements they are trying to get under way. They must count me out.

What we don't need, I feel sure, is groups, movements, banners and marches. Can we please be excused another round of exclusive and self-indulgent 'consciousness-raising'? It was bad enough the first time. Let's, for God's sake, be spared a further deepening of the notions and strategic apothegms of gender conflict. What we don't need is any more of the idea that the interests and natures of men and women are automatically antagonistic. No more sex war, chaps, we beg you.

What we do most sorely need, I urge, is abundantly more tolerance, sympathy and kindness between men and women: more affection, generosity, love. It would be a great start if we could acknowledge that, while adult life in modern times may not be a gift of sublime perfection for women, it may also be less than immaculate in its polish for men. We need binocular vision rather than the monocular squint which feminism has given us. We need to accommodate the twin recognitions that men may be subjected to specific and general disadvantages of their own; and that those disadvantages and the specific and general disadvantages of women may be relieved if we can recognise that their interests are complementary, mutual and inseparable. If we can admit that, for the time being at least, males are going to be born in roughly the same numbers as females and that the rule of nature may survive our own times and those of our children, we might as well come to terms with the reality that we are all, men and women, equally in this together.

If we start looking for an end to sex war and try to discover the mutuality of understanding we require, we may glimpse an instance of that understanding through what has come to be known as the 'glass ceiling'.

Professional women have been complaining for more than a decade about the existence of a 'glass ceiling' which obstructs their way to top jobs. That such an obstruction or difficulty exists is evident. You can see it clearly in the professions of the law, where slightly more women than men are admitted to law schools but men vastly outnumber women in senior positions, especially recorderships and judgeships.

You can see it in the medical profession. Roughly equal numbers of men and women have been received into medical schools and into the profession for nearly twenty years. At consultant level, however, men outnumber women by ten to one.

Why?

Babies.

Women leave their jobs to have babies and raise children. Men stay at their jobs and get promoted. By the time the women return to their careers, the boys have moved on. The women may even find it difficult to come back into the profession at the level at which they left it. Their chances of promotion to the top levels are minimal. They feel angry and frustrated to think that their abilities will never be fully employed.

What is the solution to this predicament offered by a political establishment which has, on this subject, been thoroughly influenced by feminism?

Day-care centres. Crèches. Nannies. Au pairs. Servants. From left to right across the face of British political life, a general consensus decrees that the interests of working women are best served if somebody other than a child's parents can be made responsible for its care during the working day.

The common beliefs in this general consensus are conservative and reactionary. In effect, they keep everybody exactly where they are and, simultaneously, deny rights and pleasures of parenthood and of family to both men and women. Meanwhile, they extend the poverties of the poor, reinforcing the divisions of class between those who have salaries and property and those who have none.

The predicament of women in the medical profession and others can be seen from a point of view which encourages change if we first remove the hood of feminist prejudice. Liberated from that death's-head blinker, we can stop supposing, as a first principle, that women are always and only the ones who suffer and bleed in our social arrangements.

In the binocular vision which clears without that obstruction we may see that it is ridiculous and damaging to speak of men and women being in competition with each other. Naturally, there must be competition between professionals for seniority (or, at least, I suppose there must be: I can't see any other way to determine the apportionments of executive responsibilities). Contemporaries will compete because they want to get better jobs; but this is a competition of colleagues, not of genders.

Women will, however, continue to be at a distinct and unvaultable disadvantage in their professional careers so long as they are the only ones expected to break the progress of those careers for the sake of the children.

This disadvantage cannot be removed if women are expected to bear chief or sole responsibility for child care at the same time as they are expected to be fully at work, sharing the same career demands which men must shoulder. The equation is unsquareable: the scales of duty, responsibility and power are hopelessly imbalanced. Meanwhile, it cannot be best for the women, for the men or for their children, not best for us as a society, that both parents should be removed by the duties of work and earning from the pleasures and responsibilities of the most vital central episode in adult personal life – its recreation.

The impossible burdens for women who must work may be eased only if we see that their difficulties and dis-advantages apply equally, on the other side of their effects, to men at home and in the family. So far as I can see, the only way to extend equal rights and opportunities for advancement to women at work is to ensure that men are as likely as women to need particular concessions from the demands of work during the time when their children are very young. By extension, this must mean that the parental rights of men in families must be considered equal to those of women. The imbalance of rights and duties on the marital see-saw may be evened only if concessions are made at both ends.

The life of the father in the family must always be nugatory so long as his rights within the family are a decorative aside and so long as he is broadly expected to be fully occupied with and chiefly interested in paid work. Men may hardly be good fathers, fully attentive to their children and providing for all their needs, emotional and material, so long as the style of life which they are expected to follow allows them meanly restricted time – or 'access' – with their children. Throughout our social and economic arrangements, a consistent general pattern can be discerned which denies to men the time to be with their children and the power to exercise that preference, if they choose it.

How may it be possible for a man to be more than a charitable uncle to his children, distributing occasional treats and sweets, if he must be at work throughout their infancies for forty, forty-eight, fifty or more hours a week? The British man, we know, is expected to work longer hours for less pay than any of his counterparts in major industrial countries in the European Community. If he must get up to go to work while his children are asleep and stay at work until they have gone to bed in the evening, he may have no waking connection with them except at weekends, when he is likely to be so tired – or so occupied with extra work to do at home – that he may be pushed to find the energy or the concentration to make an hour of play with them.

Many feminists assume that men who are fathers are content with this allowance of time with their children and seek no more. It may, indeed, be true of many millions of men that they are happiest at work and see the home and the family as a theatre of alien powers and duties which they are glad to escape; but those men are not all men, however much it may suit the hoods to think so.

239

It should be counted among the more signal inequities of our age that men who do wish or would wish to have more time with their babies or infants are given impossibly limited freedom to exercise that choice. They are given no encouragement, no honour, no power; and no time. All men are confined by the general presumption and prejudice, fostered and confirmed by a powerful strand of modern feminism, that they are, at best, reluctant parents. Men who do see themselves as enthusiastic fathers, eager to share the duties and joys of caring for their infants, are likely to find themselves hemmed in by a ring-fence of custom and practice which amounts to a comprehensive prohibition. They are not likely to be allowed to be the fathers they would wish to be.

Do you doubt that claim? Does it seem to you to be implausible that in a so-called 'male-dominated' society, a patriarchy, a man is not allowed to be father to his children as he may wish and choose? If you think that men automatically get their own way in all conditions and circumstances of family and professional life in our society, you have to ask yourself why it should be that they so infrequently get what they ask for in the divorce courts.

Look at those courts. See what the law assigns to men, by way of orders for 'access', to fathers who wish to keep a close connection with their children after separation and divorce, those who want to have an active share in their care and upbringing and who can provide them with rooms and homes. Those men may, if they are lucky, be granted what the courts are pleased to deem 'substantial' access.

What do you think 'substantial' means? Do you think it means that the father will be treated as a parent with equal affection for the child and as much right to care for the child as the mother? Do you think it might mean that the child will be with the father for approximately half the time – say,

240

Friday to Sunday evening of every week with a night in the middle? Or for six months in every year? Let me tell you what it might mean.

The granting of 'substantial access' may mean that the father will be allowed to have his children to stay with him for two Saturday nights a month. He may be given the right to meet the children from school one afternoon a week and give them their supper. And he may be allowed to have the children stay with him for a week during each of the Christmas and Easter holidays and a fortnight in the summer. I have known these arrangements for access to be called 'substantial'.

Those arrangments, determined by the courts, give a substantial picture of our collective view of fathers and their importance. The courts' adjudications and apportionments of time with the children when marriages break down provide us with a fair impress of the position given to men *within* marriage or extra-marital parental arrangements. Fathers' rights are not merely secondary: they are peripheral, marginal, decorative. Men as fathers are held to be emotional accessories to the main business of child care which is seen, by hoods and whigged judges alike, as being the essential concern of womankind.

This cast of mind towards the divisions of child care between mothers and fathers cannot survive. It is not only inequitable: it is also impractical, impolitic and damaging. In an age when women are required to be at work in the same numbers as men – which must be counted an irreversible change – it must redound to the professional disadvantage of women if they are expected to be chiefly responsible for children; and it must be counted an intolerable injustice that men are not allowed to be equally active partners in parenthood when they want to be.

The instrument by which the 'glass ceiling' might be

shattered is not to be found, therefore, in the provision of child-care facilities; but it may result, automatically, from a redistribution of the rights and responsibilities of men in the family. If men are made equal at home, women may be made equal at work.

If men and women are both, equally, expected to do much less work when their babies are born and during the years of their children's infancies, the professional disadvantages of women disappear. They evaporate. If both men and women are entitled to equal rights of leave from work and all the concessions and encouragements a modern society can provide by way of tax breaks, subsidies, subventions and honours, women would be less frantic in trying to resolve the demands of family and career and, in consequence, men would be allowed to be more attentive and loving fathers.

If we lived – as we should, and I think, must – in a society which honoured parenthood more than career title, the child-eschewing careerist might not be so full of his or her titular grandeur. If we can arrange our finances and fiscal policies – as we should and, I think, must – so that those young parents can laugh in the faces of the childless careerist and say 'We never had it so good as when we were looking after our kids', the glass ceiling might be seen as a crystal dance-floor.

How can this society be achieved? How can it be funded?

Some mighty heavy social engineering is required, with earth-movers and excavators and all hands. The riggings and the fixings of the juggernaut of state will have to be reset so that it does not roll over families but lifts and carries them. The solutions are, I believe, within our powers to execute. The resources of labour that are needed can be discovered and deployed. Our present view of our economic circumstances and future is proscribed, in part, as a result of our general reduction or exclusion of the interests of men in families.

If we can agree that young men and women of child-bearing age should be allowed more time to look after their children, we will have to agree that they should be given more money to do less work. It may follow from this principle that older people should do more work. That equation, baldly expressed, may appear to be implausible; but if you consider some of the demographic realities of our age it doesn't appear to be inconceivable.

The largest resource of labour in the next half-century will be found in the post-war generation of baby-boomers, now beginning to edge towards early retirement. The labour, fiscal and child-care requirements of our society in the next fifty years cannot be met unless this generation will take a new share of economic life, unimagined by our parents. We may not, as they did, expect to get our cards at fifty-five, sixty, sixty-five and turn them in for a twenty-year stretch of retirement in inactivity. We are going to have to do some work.

My generation of forty and fifty somethings is, in fact, already showing some signs of enthusiasm for the changed demands which we are already feeling. Middle-aged men and women are already beginning to take advantage of the very limited opportunities presently available for retraining in new occupations and professions. Redundant executives and women emerging from the years of their maternity are toying with the idea that they might become teachers, under the government's scheme for short-term training. They are signing up for courses of training in the new technologies and in old crafts and they seem to be smiling in front of their easels.

The present toying level of this tremulous development will have to be toughened and deepened. Middle-aged people contemplating retirement and thinking that they might spend a few hours a week driving the school-bus or

243

patrolling the school-crossing will need to be encouraged to lift their sights and see themselves, for perhaps half the week, in front of the blackboard or running departments in schools. Those who thought they might work a few hours at a supermarket check-out for pin money will need to be encouraged to start, run or manage their own supermarkets, entering cooperative partnerships on part-time arrangements to manage the effort. All professions are going to have to streamline their training and qualifying procedures to allow the admission of middle-aged people, already experienced in work, and give them significant duties and responsibilities. Some degree of admission to the practice of law, medicine, teaching and industrial management is going to have to be contrived after months or short years of training.

Young people who want to have children must be lavished with every form of encouragement we can provide in order that they may care for their children themselves. The state is a poor mother and a mean father. The state has no love to give because love cannot be raised in taxes nor dispensed by officials. Love is not the business of the state. It is the private work of individuals.

We can help young parents. Governments must apply some radical intelligence to their immense powers of social engineering and ease, thereby, the pains of parents who want to look after their own children. Governments must extend the munificence of tax breaks to employers who give equal rights of maternity and paternity leave. They may, via subsidy and tax advantage, give active encouragement to employers and couples who work out job-sharing arrangements. If, meanwhile, tax concessions and improved benefits were available to both men and women when they want to care for their own babies, we might begin to see some real change in the position of women at work, of men at home and of children presently in the care of others.

Employers must do more to take advantage of the capacities of new technologies and promote work to be done at home. The fax-card and the modem on the PC have turned any space in a family home into a potential work-space. Employers are unwilling to believe that they can get their money's-worth from workers at home. They imagine that, unless they can crack the whip over the workers' desks, their employees will be bunking off to walk the dog or to sneak a quick screw. As one has chosen to work at home and loves the life, I can testify that the sorest difficulty is to regulate the hours of work so one may get away from it. People who work at home tend to keep at it night and day, weekend and public holiday. They need imposed and regulated hours of rest, not of work.

All these measures are, however, trifling tinklings with the problems we face – how to manage the labour market and how to care for our children. Triflings are likely to be the best we get, as governments fudge and mudge their way through the difficulties ahead. There is, nevertheless, a truly radical option available for consideration. There is one measure in the powers of government which might settle these deeply troubling problems and failures of care in one go.

If we want to see men and women taking care of their own children, the most radical approach would be simply to halve the hours of the working week. If the legal maximum number of hours an employer can demand from an employee were twenty, rather than the forty, forty-eight, fifty which are allowable around the West today, our society would, instantly, be revolutionised in all its aspects, most particularly in child care. If a couple could support a household and their children on two incomes derived from twenty hours' work each, they could sympathetically and efficiently divide the duties of child care. Meanwhile, the change in employment law would take care of our horrible problems of unemployment among the young and the redundancy of the elderly. If employers were prohibited by law from demanding more than half a week's labour from their employees, they would have to employ other people. The pool of unemployed among the young and the retired would be mopped up at once.

What about our profits? the corporate managers will be screaming. The answer is, chaps, that something has got to give; and it's your turn. The god of profit must be toppled from its plinth: the god of love deserves more collective worship, both in the home and in the finance department. I'm not saying that you can't make a profit; I'm just saying that you're going to have to make do and manage on a lot less of it. You'll have plenty of time to think about the ways to achieve this management while you are at home with the babies.

While we dream on the radical reorganisation of our society as it must take shape in the coming century, a few simpler remedies for our immediate difficulties may be effected. The social and familial position of men can be modified by simple measures of legislation. All the disadvantages for men which I listed in the Prologue can be eliminated next year, not next century.

This process of reform has, already, tentatively begun. The earth has shifted a little under the feet of men even in the year I have been working on this book. The introduction of the Children Act 1991 will extend some rights of paternity to unmarried men, though its terms are indistinct and the Act gives no clear impression of the way the courts will be expected to perform. While the Act confirms that unmarried mothers shall continue to retain parental responsibility for the child, it allows the possibility that an unmarried father may acquire parental responsibility 'in accordance with the provisions of this Act'. We shall see how that expression works in practice. I do not doubt that the rights of unmarried fathers will be fully asserted and conformed in law before the end of this decade.

The admission of men to rights and duties of responsibility in abortion is likely to be a much more hectically vexed question. The sisterhood may be expected to resist this change to its last breath since it would admit an interest which they have always denied as their first and essential territorial claim.

On this issue, in my belief, the sisterhood has acted against the interests of women as an incidental consequence of their assault upon men. They have created the conditions in which a women bears all responsibility, moral and emotional, for a decision and an act which is gruesomely painful in its execution and its consequences. Women who choose to have an abortion might be a good deal better off if their men were required in law to endorse and to support their decision. If the men do not agree with the decision they ought to be provided with a means to say so. Their opinion ought, at least, to be registered and recorded. I'm not saying that it ought to have any restraining force in law. I'm not saying that a woman should be prevented from having an abortion if the father disapproves. I'm just saying that he has a right to be heard.

When, therefore, a woman goes to request an abortion, she should be asked if she knows the name of the father and if she is willing to give it. If she will name him, the man should be asked whether or not he agrees with the abortion or has required it. If that is his position, the fact should be recorded; and the burden of responsibility for the abortion will be shared. If he does not agree, if the abortion is being sought against his wishes, his dissent should be noted. That's all.

Women who are determined to have an abortion against the desires of the father will, of course, simply refuse to name him, excluding him from the process of consultation. Those women ought to expect to get a tougher time from the doctors. They should not be entitled, by right, to deny an elementary right to another. They should be made aware that they are acting against the interests of the broader society and that they cannot expect that society to abandon its wider responsibilities simply because those responsibilities are getting in the way of the woman's right to choose for herself and her baby.

Changes in the practices of the divorce courts are occurring and more are, clearly, in the offing. The Children Act, again, is likely to make it much easier for divorcing fathers to keep a connection with their children and to execute rights and responsibilities of care. By the end of this decade, I expect, we will no longer be seeing children in millions losing all contact with their divorcé fathers and a hundred thousand cheers may be raised at the prospect.

The rights of men to leave from work when a baby is born may be expected to be ratified in statute soon. Britain remains one of the only countries in the developed world where men still have no rights of paternity leave; but it can't last. The laws of the EC will require adjustments to be made in line in the United Kingdom. My own view is that rights of parental leave must be absolutely equal for men and women.

The sisterhood treats this claim as an outrageous denial of the special needs of women in the giving of birth and the sympathetic treatment of the post-natal period. It is no such thing. Those special needs should be endorsed and confirmed. The person who is most likely to give them sympathetic and energetic attention is the father of the child. Those attentions can only be provided in due measure if men are given extensive rights of leave. Where they exist in private corporate practice, our present arrangements for paternity leave are cruelly and cluelessly inadequate. A man cannot usefully serve the mother of a new baby if he is given three days off work. He cannot possibly make a loving bond with his baby if he is given less than a week at home. He might as well go off and play golf, as the sisters suppose that all men would if they were given rights of leave.

My own view is that neither parent of a new baby ought to be expected at work *at all* for a good three months after birth. That allowance would give them a reasonable period in which to settle their domestic arrangements and get to know their baby. Thereafter, parents of children under five years of age should not be expected to work more than part-time. This allowance would, infallibly, require the radical structural engineering in employment laws and practices which I have outlined; and it may be thought Utopian (that's all right: it's about time we shared a Utopian vision of the family). In its absence, we *can* afford reasonable and equal rights of parental leave.

The discriminatory law on retirement ages in Britain will soon be swept away under the requirements of European law. Its is nearly over. There is no more to say about it.

The rights of widowers with dependent children must be made equal with those of widows. This will, assuredly, happen.

Men who are dependents must be afforded social welfare benefits on the same terms as women. I imagine that this reform, too, may be expected before the end of the decade.

Some important changes are, therefore, in the pipelines of our social order. They will help to conduct men from the outer darkness of their exclusion from the family, that penumbra of neglect which I described when we began, into a position which confers some measures of respect and sympathy for their particular needs and difficulties. It is probable, in my mind, that the presumptions of the sister-hood as to the essential and unalterable nature of masculinity – barbaric, slobbish, uncivilised and unfamilial – will have withered into redundancy as active principles of definition within a few years. By the end of the century, I imagine that the harridans who have been so proud of their spite will be trilling denials at their dinner-tables: 'Oh, yes, I did once call myself a feminist because it was just the best fun a girl could have; but I was never one of those who wanted to kill men . . .' Can't you hear it?

Some of the hoods are, of course, comprehensively stuck. They have advanced themselves into positions of genuine power in commerce and media through the claims of sisterhood, upon which their self-esteem and their positions depend. They cannot be expected to cough up contrition or apology, to say 'Ooops, sorry: I did get that a bit wrong. Can we start again?' Those ladies are not going to change their tune. We can only hope that they will be left to dance to it alone until they waft away in dust.

Meanwhile, the rest of us have an almighty act of reconstruction and of reparation to make, a penance to declare and a crime of totalitarian ego to renounce. We owe our world a duty of political engagement and of service to the young whose minds we have confused and whose lives we have intolerably burdened and frustrated. If we can put behind us the sex war divisions and the casuistries of sexual terror to which we have submitted, we may, in our post-menopausal, post-reproductive years, have a chance to fulfil the political, artistic and libertarian promise of our youth and, at last, be an improving presence on the earth in our own time. There is a little of that time left. Enough, I trust.

Now we may perhaps begin? What do you say?